IN THE KNOW IN

Germany

W0010395

LIVING LANGUAGE®

TERRA COGNITA™

Also available from

Business Companion: German

This essential language guide for working with German colleagues is a perfect complement to *In the Know in Germany*. The 416-page handbook contains more than 1,000 phrases for general business situations and vocabulary for over 25 specific industries, plus a two-way glossary, and handy reference sections. The audio CD contains more than 500 phrases used in realistic business situations.

Handbook/CD program 0-609-60682-4 $21.95/C$32.95
Handbook only 0-609-80627-0 $12.95/C$19.95

German Complete Course
For beginners or those who want a thorough review

Our best-selling program will have you speaking German in just six weeks. Developed by U.S. government experts, it features a proven speed-learning method that progresses from words to phrases to complete sentences and dialogues. Includes a course-book, a dictionary, and 40 lessons on two 90-minute cassettes or three 60-minute CDs.

Cassette program 1-4000-2006-9 $25.00/C$38.00
CD program 1-4000-2007-7 $25.00/C$38.00
Coursebook only 1-4000-2008-5 $8.00/C$12.00
Dictionary only 1-4000-2009-3 $5.95/C$8.95

Ultimate German: Basic-Intermediate

A comprehensive program equivalent to two years of college-level study. Up-to-date conversations and vocabulary in each lesson teach reading, writing, grammar, and culture tips along with conversational skills. Includes a coursebook and more than 40 lessons on eight 60-minute cassettes or CDs. An advanced course is also available.

Cassette program 0-609-60760-X $75.00/C$115.00
CD program 0-609-60733-2 $75.00/C$115.00
Coursebook only 0-609-80680-7 $18.00/C$27.50

Available at bookstores everywhere
www.livinglanguage.com

300 West 49th Street Suite 314 New York, New York 10019 USA
Phone: 212.663.9890 Fax: 212.663.2404
E-mail: info@terracognita.com
www.terracognita.com

Know Your World

Terra Cognita provides top quality cross-cultural training service and resources. The goal of our cross-cultural learning material is to help you build the awareness and skills to recognize and respect cultural differences you will encounter. Terra Cognita programs thereby ensure a sucessful adjustment to life in a new culture for expatriates and the skills necessary to succeed in international business.

Terra Cognita delivers cross-cultural learning with private seminars and workshops, with online learning modules, and with a variety of video, audio and printed material. Currently Terra Cognita programs meet the needs of expatriates and international business colleagues at various multinational companies, government agencies and educational institutions worldwide.

 LIVE ABROAD! is an innovative video-based expatriate preparation program that covers the entire expatriate experience from preparing to go through the cultural adjustment process to the final return home.

 WORK ABROAD! is a video-based program that explains and vividly re-creates the cross-cultural dynamics of the international business environment.

For more information on Terra Cognita
and a wealth of articles and resources for cross-cultural learning,
visit our Web site at WWW.TERRACOGNITA.COM

V I D E O S   S E M I N A R S   O N L I N E

LIVING LANGUAGE®

A Random House Company

IN THE KNOW IN

Germany

THE INDISPENSABLE CROSS-CULTURAL GUIDE TO WORKING AND LIVING IN GERMANY

WRITTEN BY

Jennifer Phillips

EDITED BY

Christopher Warnasch

Terra Cognita

Published in the United States by Living Language, A Random House Company

www.livinglanguage.com

Design by Barbara M. Bachman
Illustrations by Adrian Hashimi

Although all factual information in this book, such as Web sites, telephone
numbers, etc., is as up-to-date as possible at press time, changes occur all
the time, and Living Language cannot accept responsibility for the accuracy
of the facts in the book or for inadvertent errors or omissions.

First Paperback Edition

ISBN 1-4000-2046-8

Library of Congress Cataloging-in-Publication Data available

PRINTED IN THE UNITED STATES OF AMERICA

10 9 8 7 6 5 4 3 2 1

ACKNOWLEDGMENTS

Special thanks to Stefanie Carillo, who provided invaluable assistance in interviewing, researching, and tracking down the answers to an endless stream of questions. Thanks as well to the people who generously shared their experiences and input, and to my editor, Chris Warnasch, for his expert guidance. No book is written in a vacuum, and this one would never have happened without the generous support of Richard Davis, with whom I continue a journey toward Terra Cognita. And finally, last on this list, but not in my heart, to Jan, who provided the occasional much-needed kick in the seat, and to my family for their support and encouragement.

And thanks to the rest of the Living Language team: Lisa Alpert, Elizabeth Bennett, Helen Tang, Elyse Tomasello, Zviezdana Verzich, Suzanne McGrew, Pat Ehresmann, Denise DeGennaro, Linda Schmidt, Marina Padakis, and Barbara Bachman.

CONTENTS

CONTENTS

CONTENTS

CONTENTS

Whether you're moving to Germany or traveling there for business, it's essential that you know what to expect, and what will be expected of you. Cross-cultural awareness provides you with just that knowledge. Living Language® and Terra Cognita™ *In the Know in Germany* is designed to help both businesspeople and their families navigate the often complex waters of life in another culture. By culture we don't mean Wagner's *Lohengrin* or the philosophies of Kant and Hegel. Culture is the backdrop of every activity you engage in and every word you exchange. In Germany, you'll be dealing with a foreign culture every time you shake a colleague's hand, sit down to write an e-mail, get on a train, or even buy a loaf of bread. A list of "dos and don'ts" provides only part of the picture. A more thorough understanding of culture—what really motivates people's behaviors, attitudes, beliefs, and habits—will allow you, and any family members with you, to adapt with ease to both the social and business environments of Germany.

This book was developed to be easy, practical, and comprehensive. You'll first get your bearings through some general background information about Germany, such as its history, geography, political system, and social structure. This is no history text, though. The Background section is meant to be a brief survey that will familiarize you with some important landmarks you'll no doubt hear about or see. If something strikes you as interesting, the Background section will also serve you well as a way to get your feet wet in a particular area; we leave any further exploration of German history to you.

Next you'll read an overview of German culture. For our purposes here, we've broken culture down into the following six categories: Time, Communication, Group Dynamics, Status and Hierarchy, Relationships, and Reasoning. Naturally, this provides only a general picture of the components of German culture, but a very practical picture, too. And even while using these generalizations, we can never forget that any culture is made up of individuals, and individuals vary. Learning about these important general concepts, though, where differences and pitfalls abound, will better prepare you and your family for a more successful experience abroad.

The next section, Living Abroad, is meant to give you some insight into the issues that people face in other cultures. Here you'll learn what to expect as an individual: a businessperson, a family member, a parent, a child, or a teenager. This section applies to life in any other culture, and you'll find the insights invaluable. It will raise the kinds of important questions you'll want to consider when preparing to make an adjustment to life abroad. Most importantly, it will prepare you to face some tough challenges, and then reap some wonderful benefits.

The next two sections of the book, Getting Around and Living and Staying in Germany, are a comprehensive, step-by-step guide to everyday life in Germany. These are the issues that everyone must deal with, from driving and taking buses to shopping, waiting in line, and social etiquette. These sections are full of clearly organized information, practical lists, and essential tips. Everyone—single traveler, parent, or child—will benefit.

Next are two sections designed specifically for the businessperson. In Business Environment, you'll get an idea of the general principles that govern working in Germany, from company values and structure to chain of command, unions, workspace, and women in business. In the next section, Business Step-by-Step, you'll learn about the real essentials of doing business in Germany, ranging from such important issues as dress, speeches and presentations, and negotiations, to such often overlooked but crucial details as business-card etiquette and making appointments.

Finally, we leave you with an introduction to the essentials of the German language. While it is true that English is the lingua franca of global business, it cannot be denied that even a very basic knowledge of a foreign language can make a world of difference. This is no full-service language course; you won't be memorizing any irregular verbs or grammar rules. But you'll find that the minimal amount of time it takes to learn some basic social expressions and survival vocabulary will be recouped a hundred times over. Your German colleagues and friends will be very appreciative that you've made an effort to learn just a little of their language. You'll find that the experience of another language is often its own reward, and you may even want to go further and learn to speak German more fluently.

Good luck! (or *Viel Glück!*) and enjoy. We hope you find this coverage informative, practical, and enriching.

BACKGROUND

Germany is one of the most industrialized nations in Europe and boasts one of the highest standards of living in the world. In addition, it is a leading member of the European Union and host to many multinational companies, making it a formidable economic power.

Some Americans feel that the culture of Germany, like that of most western European countries, isn't different enough from their own to bother learning about. They couldn't be more wrong, as many have learned to their detriment. In fact, any time that you plan to live or do business in another country, you cannot help but benefit from foreknowledge of the country and its culture. Not only will you be a more effective businessperson, you will also come out of the experience understanding your own culture—and yourself—on a deeper level.

But for now, let's start with the basics.

VITAL STATISTICS

The following information is based on the latest available data at the time of publication.

Official Name:	**Bundesrepublik Deutschland (Federal Republic of Germany)**
Capital:	**Berlin (some government offices remain in Bonn, the seat of government of West Germany prior to reunification, until they can be transferred to Berlin)**
Federal Flag:	**Black, red, and gold horizontal tricolor**
Federal Seal:	**Black eagle on gold background**
National Anthem:	**Third stanza of the Deutschlandlied**
Area:	**137,826 square mi (356,970 square km)**
Land Distribution:	**54.1% farming; 29.4% forest; 11.8% developed, roads, railways; 2.2% water; 2.5% other**
Highest Point:	**The Zugspitze in the Bavarian Alps (9,718 ft)**
Lowest Point:	**Freepsum Lake, -6 feet**
Natural Resources:	**Iron ore, coal, timber, copper, natural gas, salt**
Population (2002 est.):	**83.2 million**
Male life expectancy:	**73**

Female life expectancy:	81
Population Density (2000):	595 per square mi
Population Growth (2002 est.):	0.26%
Urban/Rural Distribution:	14.7% live in the twelve largest cities
Average Family Size:	2.3 members (1.71 children per family)
Largest Cities:	Berlin, Hamburg, Munich
Ethnicity:	91.5% Germans; 2.4% Turks; 6.19% other (Danes, Italians, former Yugoslav nationals, Greeks, Africans, Poles, and others)
Language:	German; Sorbian and Danish minorities
Literacy:	99%
Religions:	38% Protestant (Lutheran, Reformed, and United); 34% Roman Catholic; 1.7% Muslim; 26.3% other (mainly Jewish and agnostic)
Currency:	Euro
GDP (2001):	$2.174 trillion
Major Trading Partners:	European Union, led by France (56.4% of exports, 54.2% of imports); United States (9.3% of exports, 8.2% of imports); Japan (1.9% of exports, 5.0% of imports)
Per Capita Income (2001):	$26,200

Inflation (2001):	2.4%
Unemployment (2001):	9.4%
Employment by Industry:	56% services; 40% industry; 4% agriculture, forestry, fishing

For the most recent figures, visit
www.odci.gov/cia/publications/factbook/index.html

GEOGRAPHY AND CLIMATE

Situated in the heart of Europe, Germany has for many years served as a link between western Europe and central and eastern Europe. With over 82 million inhabitants, Germany has Europe's second-highest population, topped only by that of Russia. Despite having a larger population, Germany is smaller than both France and Spain.

Germany is home to a wide variety of landscapes, ranging from the plains of the north to the towering Alps in the south. Germany's topography can be divided into five areas from north to south: the northern German plain, the central upland range, the terraced southwest, the southern Alpine foothills, and the Bavarian Alps.

Most of Germany is moderately cool year round. Temperatures range from lows between −6°and 2°C (23°and 35°F) in the winter to summer highs of 18° to 30°C (65°–85°F). While summers are sunny and warm, they are usually not hot enough to require air conditioning, and most homes do not have it. Similarly, although winters see some snow, most of the country does not experience extreme cold. The exceptions are the Bavarian Alps, the Hartz Mountains in Lower Saxony, parts of the Black Forest, and the higher-altitude regions of northern Franconia, which experience colder winters and heavier snowfall. The southern regions of Bavaria also experience from time to time the *Föhn*, a warm Alpine wind. This can occur in any season, and bring with it clear, warm weather—not to mention sudden atmospheric pressure changes and often a twilight that can be extraordinarily beautiful in the Munich area.

Each of Germany's different regions has a beauty all its own. Each is worthy of a visit. Some of the more notable areas are:

The Bavarian Alps

A range of dramatic, fir-covered mountains, the Bavarian Alps border Austria. Quaint towns filled with traditional half-timbered houses (complete with window sills full of colorful flowers) and the architectural creations of Mad King Ludwig II are some of the sights to see. Did you know that King Ludwig's castle Neuschwanstein was the model for Cinderella Castle at Walt Disney World?

Der Schwarzwald (The Black Forest)

Known to foreigners for its namesake cake and cuckoo clocks, the Black Forest is also where you will find the healing waters of Germany's most famous spas, including renowned Baden-Baden. Away from the trendy spa areas, however, is a beautiful forest setting with a village atmosphere. The dense firs and evergreens that fill the forests are what give the area its well-deserved name.

Die Romantische Straße (The Romantic Road)

The Romantic Road (admittedly staked out with the tourist in mind) takes you south from Würzburg in Lower Bavaria to Füssen on the Austrian border. Along the way you have the opportunity to stop at some of Europe's most fabulous rococo castles, a medieval village or two, splendid cathedrals, and at least one Renaissance city. Near the end of the road, you have a second opportunity to visit King Ludwig's fantasy castle Neuschwanstein.

Die Märchenstraße (The Fairy-Tale Road)

This route (another popular track for tourists) travels from Hanau, just east of Frankfurt, to Bremen, some 370 miles to the north. As you wind your way northward, you pass through countless picturesque villages, each full of half-timbered houses and most with castles. Hanau is the birthplace of the Grimm brothers, and this is truly the Germany that comes to mind as you read "Hansel and Gretel" and other fairy tales. Most of the 65 towns along the way have theater performances of the Grimms' tales, and you can find many restaurants with historical settings.

The Rhineland

One of the most popular trips in Germany is a boat ride down the Rhine River, lined with magnificent castles and miles of vine-covered banks. A quick side trip down the Mosel River, a tributary of the Rhine, takes you to Trier, Germany's oldest city. There are many castles along the Rhine with accommodations and great restaurants inside.

You can find more information on sites like these on the Internet at: www.germany-tourism.de and www.fodors.com/germany.

PEOPLE AND LIFE

Germany is one of Europe's most densely populated countries. Berlin and its surroundings and other large metropolitan areas such as Frankfurt, Hamburg, Dresden, and Munich are heavily populated, in direct contrast to the north German plains region, sections of Mecklenberg–Western Pomerania, and a few other areas. Once outside the big cities, you quickly come to vast regions dotted by small towns and even smaller villages. And even most big cities contain a kernel of their small-town past embodied in the *Altstadt* (old city), a district with the atmosphere of long-ago Germany, often complete with at least a few cobblestone streets.

Germany's population is 92% German. The country evolved from a number of Germanic tribes, including the Franks, Saxons, Bavarians, and Swabians. As you travel throughout Germany, you will still notice some differences in their customs and traditions, and especially in their festivals and celebrations. Another notable difference is in the dialects of the various regions of Germany. Unlike the many regional accents in the United States, German dialects to some extent have their own vocabulary, syntax, and even grammatical structure. While they are not quite separate languages, Germans from different regions would sometimes have difficulty understanding each other were they to speak in their home dialects. Luckily, Germany also has a standard language, called *Hochdeutsch* (High German), which is taught in schools. If you are living in Germany, however, you will have to tune your ear to the local dialect, as it is what you will hear in shops, in casual conversation, and in homes. There is no difference between dialects in the written language, except perhaps for a few regional idioms.

The states that make up modern Germany were created after World War II in agreement with the occupying powers. As such they are political divisions and were not drawn with ethnic distinctions in mind. However, Germans tend to identify with their region, not necessarily their state. For example, they will refer to themselves as Swabian (Swabia is a rather indefinite area in southern Germany, roughly centered around Stuttgart), rather than natives of Baden-Württemberg, the state in which they live.

Like many people, Germans have their own stereotypes about each other. For example, folks from Mecklenberg are characterized as being reserved, Swabians are known for their thrift, Saxons are hard workers, Rhinelanders are the most carefree, and Bavarians are the most laid-back of the bunch. You should naturally take these stereotypes with a grain of salt, as you would the regional stereotypes from your own country.

Two non-German ethnic groups comprise a small minority of Germany's population. These are the Lusatian Sorbs, descendants of Slavic tribes who settled near the Elbe and Saale rivers in the 6th century, and the Frisians, descendants of a Germanic tribe from the North Sea coastal area. Both have their own language and cultural traditions but have been integrated into the German population. A small Danish population is also found in Schleswig-Holstein, the state that borders Denmark.

In addition to the above groups, Germany is host to several foreign communities. The largest is the Turkish population, followed by immigrants from the former Yugoslavia. Italians, Greeks, Austrians, and natives of all other European countries can be found in Germany, as can people from various African countries.

The German at Home

Whereas the typical American will move a number of times during his or her life, Germans tend to stay put. Many Germans continue to live in or near the town in which they grew up. There are many reasons for this. For one thing, German workers do not switch jobs as frequently as Americans do. Although lifetime employment is not by any means guaranteed, many different facets of the business environment combine to ensure that the majority of workers remain with one employer. In addition, families are an important part of German life, and people tend not to move too far from immediate relatives. A modicum of regional pride and loyalty also plays a part.

During leisure time, which is considerable thanks to a short work week and a liberal vacation policy, a German can often be found around the home, gardening or doing handiwork, engaging in some type of athletic activity such as cycling or hiking, or just relaxing. Clubs exist for every type of sport or activity imaginable, as well as youth and women's organizations, and there are few Germans who don't belong to at least one club. If you are an equestrian, an art lover, a camper, or a chess player, you will find a place in a local club.

Germans are also renowned globetrotters. Many people take their vacation time (four weeks or more) as a block, and plan international excursions. Southern climes such as Italy and Greece, South America, and the United States are popular destinations for the German tourist.

IMPORTANT ISSUES

Reunification

For the past decade, reunification has been in the forefront of most people's minds. The dream of a reunited Germany brought with it the reality of a host of problems. The more prosperous former West Germany found itself bolstering the collapsed economy of the former East Germany as unemployment rose. In the years since the 1949 division, the gulf between the two Germanies had grown in many ways. Technology, wages, and the availability of goods in East Germany all lagged behind West Germany. The East German workforce suffered as newer technologies were introduced, both because of its lack of training in them and because they meant fewer workers were required. Even today, remnants of tension between the two former Germanies can be found at times. Some western Germans resent carrying the burden of the less advanced eastern states. People in the eastern states also felt the pangs of reunification, knowing that they were the dependent partners in the process.

Gastarbeiter (Guest Workers)

Following World War II, Germany welcomed foreigners as a solution to its shortage of workers needed to rebuild and sustain its economy. The first Gastarbeiter were Italians, but they soon included Greeks, Spaniards, Portuguese, Yugoslavs, and Turks. Turks eventually overtook other nationalities as the largest foreign population. Now over half of the foreigners residing in Germany have been there for over ten years, and more than two-thirds of their children were born there. When Germany's economy took a downturn and unemployment began to rise, the *Gastarbeiter* became the subject of controversy. Feelings about Germany's minority residents today remain mixed. On the one hand, they are willing to take on many of the jobs that many Germans refuse, mostly menial, low-paying jobs. On the other hand, because many of those same people have family "back home," much of their income flows outside of Germany's borders rather than being spent inside the country. Further controversy exists over their rights to German social services and being taught in their own language. Despite all this, Germany remains proud of its admirable history of taking in both asylum seekers and war refugees.

The Environment

Germans are among the most environmentally conscious people in the world. This can be attributed in part to Germany's position in Europe and in part to its history as an industrial nation. Because Germany sits in the center of Europe, it is affected by the environmental actions (or inaction) of its neighbors. Over a century of industry has caused major pollution problems. A 1994 addition to the German *Grundgesetz*, or Constitution, made it the duty of the state to protect the environment.

Germany's environmental policy is based on three principles: prevention; making the polluter, not the public, pay; and cooperation among government, business and private citizens to solve environmental problems.

Strict environmental regulations require all companies to control the amount of pollution they emit and to pay for any environmental damage they cause. Additional legislation requires individuals to combat pollution by using clean power and reducing car emissions. Recycling is required of everyone.

Germany has spent billions of marks on environmental initiatives. One of the biggest challenges occurred following the reunification. East Germany had few environmental control laws, so major modifications had to be made on all levels to bring the former East German industries and products up to the standards set by West Germany.

GERMAN HISTORY IN BRIEF

Germany's past is reflected in its present, so to understand Germany today one must understand its history. In Germany, great value is placed on the process of getting from one point to another with care and foresight, not just blindly racing into the future. Tomes have been written on German history, but since that is not the focus of this book, this section is limited to the highlights. If you plan to spend any significant amount of time in Germany, however, it would be a good idea to pick up a book with a more in-depth look at the country's history.

The coalescence of the German state was a process that took hundreds of years and drew together myriad Germanic tribes. An early, shadowy figure who is generally credited with beginning the process that led to German statehood was Hermann (Arminius in Latin), a prince of the Cherusci tribe, who in AD 9 conquered three Roman legions in the Teutoburg Forest. After hundreds of years of battle with the Romans, as well as tribal skirmishes, the Germanic empire reached its peak under Karl der Große (Charlemagne), so our outline begins there.

THE FIRST REICH / THE HOLY ROMAN EMPIRE

768	Karl der Große becomes king
800	Karl der Große is crowned emperor in Rome
814	Karl der Große dies in Aachen
834	The empire of Karl der Große is divided among his three grandchildren under the Treaty of Verdun; Ludwig (Louis the Pious) receives the eastern territories, but divides them into the duchies of Franconia, Saxony, Bavaria, Swabia (870), and Lorraine (900)
962	Otto I is crowned emperor in Rome and recognized by Byzantium

1075	Dispute over the right to appoint bishops (investiture) begins between Emperor Henry IV and Pope Gregory VII, marking the onset of strife between the German state and the Church
1096	Beginning of the First Crusade
1138–1254	The Hohenstaufen dynasty
1235	Emperor Frederick II proclaims the Peace of Mainz, the first imperial law in the German language
1348–1352	The plague (Black Death) kills over 25 million people throughout Europe, including more than one-third of Germany's population
1452	Coronation of Frederick III, the last German emperor, in Rome
1495	Proclamation of the "Eternal Peace" at the diet (general assembly of estates) of Worms
1517	Martin Luther nails his Ninety-Five Theses to the door of the church in Wittenberg, marking the beginning of the Reformation

REFORMATION

1524–1525	Peasants' War
1555	The Peace of Augsburg, which allows princes to determine the religion of their respective territories
1618	The beginning of the Thirty Years' War; the Peace of Westphalia (1648) ends the war

THE SECOND REICH

1701	Frederick III of Brandenburg crowns himself King Frederick I of Prussia
1740	Frederick the Great crowned king of Prussia; first Silesian War between Prussia and Austria (ended 1742)
1744–1745	Second Silesian War
1806	Napoléon forms the Confederation of the Rhine and destroys the remnants of the Holy Roman Empire; Francis II, the Emperor, claims the title Emperor of Austria instead
1813–1815	Wars against France to gain liberation from Napoléon
1815	Founding of the German Confederation at the Congress of Vienna
1850	Prussian Constitution implemented
1862	Bismarck becomes prime minister of Prussia
1866	War between Austria and Prussia leads to the dissolution of the German Confederation
1871	German Empire is founded by Otto von Bismarck, who becomes Reich's Chancellor; Wilhelm I crowned emperor in Versailles
1890	Wilhelm II dismisses Otto von Bismarck
1914	Outbreak of World War I, which leads to the destruction of the Second Reich

THE THIRD REICH & DIVISION

1919	Peace Treaty of Versailles; Weimar Republic is established
1923	Massive inflation following the war
1925	Paul von Hindenburg is elected Reich's President
1933	Von Hindenburg appoints Adolf Hitler Reich's Chancellor
1935	Anti-Jewish Nuremberg Laws enacted
1939	Germany and Soviet Union agree to non-aggression pact; Germany then attacks Poland, beginning World War II
1942	The Wannsee Conference, at which the Nazi leaders decide to systematically eradicate Jews
1945	Hitler commits suicide; Germany surrenders unconditionally and is occupied by Allied troops; concentration camps are liberated; the Potsdam Conference divides Germany among the Allies; Nuremberg trials
1948	Allies end occupation; Soviet Union blockades West Berlin; American, English, and French pilots organize the Berlin Airlift
1949	The German states previously occupied by England, France, and the United States become the Federal Republic of Germany (*Bundesrepublik Deutschland*, BRD); the Soviet-occupied sector becomes the German Democratic Republic (*Deutsche Demokratische Republik*, DDR)
1961	The government of East Germany builds the Berlin Wall

REUNIFICATION

1972	Basic Treaty agreed to by the governments of East and West Germany
1989	East Germans pressure for greater freedoms and reform through demonstrations; the Berlin Wall is torn down and communist rule in East Germany collapses
1990	East Germany joins West Germany; Berlin becomes the capital of unified Germany

NOTED (AND NOTORIOUS) GERMANS

In the Arts & Philosophy

JOHANN SEBASTIAN BACH, 1685–1750
Now celebrated as a sublime composer, Bach was better known as an organist during his lifetime. Bach's body of work includes instrumental and orchestral suites, oratorios, concertos, and more than 300 sacred cantatas.

LUDWIG VAN BEETHOVEN, 1770–1827
Beethoven is considered one of the world's greatest composers, famous for concertos, sonatas, and quartets in addition to his nine major symphonies.

MARLENE DIETRICH, 1901–1992
An internationally renowned actress, Dietrich assumed the character of the sultry femme fatale. She is probably best known for her film *The Blue Angel*.

ALBRECHT DÜRER, 1471–1528
Painter, printmaker, and theoretician, Dürer was the first German artist to win acclaim outside Germany.

RAINER WERNER FASSBINDER, 1946–1982
Fassbinder directed over 40 films portraying life in post–World War II Germany, including *The Marriage of Maria Braun, Lola,* and *Veronika Voss*.

JOHANN WOLFGANG VON GOETHE, 1749–1832
This poet, playwright, novelist, and scientist is best known for his *Faust*, considered one of the world's greatest works of literature.

GÜNTER GRASS, 1927–

Grass is known for his social criticism and political activism, seen in novels such as *The Tin Drum* and *The Flounder*. He was awarded the Nobel Prize for Literature in 1999.

GEORG FRIEDRICH HANDEL, 1685–1759

One of the most important composers of the Baroque period, Handel is most famous for his orotorio *Messiah*.

FRIEDRICH NIETZSCHE, 1844–1900

Philosopher and author of such works as *Thus Spake Zarathustra* and *Beyond Good and Evil*, Nietzsche rejected the "slave morality" of Christianity in favor of a new, heroic morality that would affirm life, led by a breed of *Übermenschen* (supermen).

RICHARD WAGNER, 1813–1883

Perhaps the foremost of the German Romantic composers, Wagner repeatedly drew on German mythology in his operas, among them *Tannhäuser, The Ring of the Nibelungs,* and *Lohengrin.*

In the Military & Government

KONRAD ADENAUER, 1876–1967

Post–World War II Germany's first chancellor, Adenauer was the architect of West German democracy.

OTTO VON BISMARCK, 1815–1898

Creator of the German Empire (the Second Reich) and its first chancellor, Bismarck consolidated the German states and attained enormous power. As chancellor, Bismarck was the real force behind the throne.

HERMANN GÖRING, 1893–1946

One of Adolf Hitler's earliest followers, Göring founded the Gestapo (secret police). Sentenced to death for his war crimes at the

Nuremberg trials, Göring committed suicide two hours before he was to be hanged.

PAUL VON HINDENBURG, 1847–1934
Hindenburg's victories as a World War I field marshal made him a war hero. Elected president in 1925, Hindenburg defeated Adolf Hitler in the 1932 elections, but became a figurehead president after appointing Hitler chancellor.

ADOLF HITLER, 1889–1945
Although born in Austria, Hitler is inextricably linked to Germany's history. Hitler served in the Bavarian army in World War I and received the Iron Cross for bravery. Embittered by Germany's defeat, which he blamed on Jews and Marxists, Hitler formed the Nazi party with other nationalists. Following his appointment as chancellor under Paul von Hindenburg in 1933, Hitler soon gained dictatorial powers and prepared Germany for war under his Third Reich. In his book *Mein Kampf*, Hitler laid the groundwork for the establishment of concentration camps and the Holocaust.

ERICH HONECKER, 1912–1994
Honecker was the leader of East Germany for 20 years before the Berlin Wall was torn down and reunification began. Extradited from Russia, Honecker was slated to stand trial for crimes perpetrated under his leadership, but was released because of poor health and died a year later in exile in Chile.

KARL DER GROßE, C. 742–814
Also claimed by the French as Charlemagne, Karl der Große was king of the Franks before being crowned as the first emperor of the Holy Roman Empire, the first German Reich.

ROSA LUXEMBURG, 1871–1919, AND
KARL LIEBKNECHT, 1871–1919
As a student, Luxemburg helped found the Polish Socialist Party. She went on to lead the German Social Democratic Party and,

together with Liebknecht, founded the Marxist Spartacus Party, the precursor of the German Communist Party. Luxemburg and Liebknecht were both arrested during the Spartacist uprising in 1919 and subsequently murdered by soldiers.

KARL MARX, 1818–1883
A social philosopher and revolutionary, Marx, together with Friedrich Engels, was the founder of modern socialism and communism. Marx collaborated with Engels in writing the *Communist Manifesto*. Exiled in London, Marx used dialectical materialism to analyze economic and social history in *Das Kapital*.

BARON MANFRED VON RICHTHOFEN, 1892–1918
The legendary "Red Baron," World War I air ace Richthofen was the leader of the "Flying Circus" that downed dozens of Allied aircraft.

In Sports

FRANZ BECKENBAUER, 1945–
Germany's favorite football (soccer) player, the "Football Kaiser" led the Bayern München team to victory in the 1974 World Cup.

BORIS BECKER, 1967–
In 1985, Becker caught the eye of the world when he became the youngest winner at the Wimbledon tennis tournament.

MICHAEL SCHUMACHER, 1969–
As Germany's leading racecar driver, Schumacher, affectionately known as "Schumi," is a national sports hero.

Other

JOHANN GUTENBERG, c.1397–1468
Although little is known about Gutenberg, this printer is credited with being the first European to print on a printing press with mov-

able type. The Gutenberg Bible, printed in Mainz before 1456, is thought to have been the first large book printed with movable type.

MARTIN LUTHER, 1483–1546

Disturbed by the Catholic Church's practice of selling indulgences, Luther determined to initiate reforms. While he sought only to eliminate corruption in the Church, his Reformation soon broadened, and the Protestant movement swelled following his excommunication in 1521. Soon afterward, he began his translation of the Bible into German.

RELIGION

Although you will find empty pews on Sunday, the majority of Germans are at least nominally either Protestant (38%) or Catholic (34%). Generally speaking, the southern regions and the Rhineland tend to have a Catholic majority, while the northern and eastern regions are mainly Protestant. The two faiths co-exist in relative harmony, along with Judaism, Islam, and smaller Christian denominations such as Mormons and Jehovah's Witnesses. Religion is largely a private matter to Germans, so religious groups who proselytize are looked at somewhat askance. Accordingly, it's not advisable to inquire about another person's religious beliefs or mention your own in the course of conversation.

Unlike the United States, Germany has no strict division of church and state. Many public holidays celebrate Christian feast days, and churches receive tax money. That said, however, churches do not exert a great deal of political clout.

POLITICS & GOVERNMENT

The Government System

Germany has a federal system of government with 16 *Länder*, or states, which form a parliamentary democracy. Much of Germany's political power lies at the regional, rather than the federal, level. All Germans are granted the right to vote at age 18.

STATE	CAPITAL
Baden-Württemberg	Stuttgart
Bayern (Bavaria)	München (Munich)
Berlin*	
Brandenburg**	Potsdam
Bremen*	
Hamburg*	
Hessen	Wiesbaden
Niedersachsen (Lower Saxony)	Hannover
Mecklenburg-Vorpommern**	Schwerin
Nordrhein-Westfalen	Düsseldorf
Rheinland-Pfalz	Mainz
Saarland	Saarbrücken
Sachsen (Saxony)**	Dresden
Sachsen-Anhalt**	Magdeburg
Schleswig-Holstein	Kiel
Thüringen (Thuringia)**	Erfurt

* City-states
** Former states in the German Democratic Republic

Germany, like the United States, has three branches of government: executive, legislative, and judicial. The American Constitution served as a model for Germany's constitution after World War II.

The Executive Branch

The executive branch consists of the *Bundespräsident* (Federal President), the *Bundeskanzler* (Federal Chancellor) and the federal ministers. As the head of government, the chancellor is the political leader of the country; the president has a primarily representational role. The president is elected to a five-year term by a special convention.

The Legislative Branch

Composed of 672 members, the *Bundestag*, the federal parliament, makes federal laws and constitutional amendments, and is responsible for determining foreign policy. The chancellor is usually the party leader of the largest party in the dominant political coalition. The *Bundestag* is elected by national vote. Voters mark their ballot once for a specific representative, then again for a party. Approximately half of the *Bundestag* seats are filled by the first, direct vote. The remaining seats are distributed among all parties that receive at least 5% of the votes; each acquires one or more seats according to the percentage of votes received. The party then fills its seat allotment from a predetermined list of candidates. In this way, smaller, but significant, political interest groups can gain a seat in the *Bundestag*. *Bundestag* elections are held once every four years; special off-year elections can be called in certain circumstances.

The second arm of the legislative branch is the *Bundesrat*. Composed of representatives from the state governments, this body allows the states to participate in legislation at the federal level. A state is accorded between three and six seats according to its population.

The Judicial Branch

The judicial branch encompasses the Federal Constitutional Court, seated in Karlsruhe, plus five additional federal courts: Court of Justice, Administrative Court, Financial Court, Labor Court, and Social Court. These five federal courts are the courts of final appeal in their respective jurisdictions. Judges are federally appointed and are chosen by a committee headed by the minister under whose jurisdiction the court falls.

Political Parties

According to German law, political parties that are able to capture at least five percent of the votes are entitled to representation in the *Bundestag*. Germany currently has six political parties holding seats in the *Bundestag*: the *Christlich-Demokratische Union Deutschlands* (CDU), the *Sozialdemokratische Partei Deutschlands* (SPD), the *Freie Demokratische Partei* (FDP), the *Christlich-Soziale Union* (CSU), *Allianz 90/Die Grünen*, and the *Partei des Demokratischen Sozialismus* (PDS).

CHRISTIAN DEMOCRATIC UNION (CHRISTLICH-DEMOKRATISCHE UNION DEUTSCHLANDS, CDU)

Following World War II, Konrad Adenauer (who was to become the first post-war chancellor) and others formed the CDU, a party based on Judeo-Christian principles and a political philosophy of a social market economy. Today the CDU enjoys the support of a wide base of the German populace, but especially business and agriculture.

CHRISTIAN SOCIAL UNION (CHRISTLICH-SOZIALE UNION, CSU)

Based on similar principles, but existing only in Bavaria, the CSU is considered the Bavarian arm of the CDU. Although largely a regional party, the CSU maintains its clout through its alliance with the CDU.

SOCIAL DEMOCRATIC PARTY (SOZIALDEMOKRATISCHE PARTEI DEUTSCHLANDS, SPD)

Germany's oldest political party, the SPD has its roots as the party of the working class. Today, however, it receives support from white-collar workers and professionals as well, and its philosophy has moved from the Marxism of its early days to liberal capitalism and the involvement of government in righting economic and social inequality. 1969 saw the election of the first SPD chancellor, Willy Brandt, who marked the beginning of an SPD-led government that lasted until 1982. During this period, the SPD established treaties with the

Soviet Union, Poland, and East Germany, heralding the beginning of the end of East-West tensions.

FREE DEMOCRATIC PARTY (FREIE DEMOKRATISCHE PARTEI, FDP)

Politically at the center of Germany's political spectrum, the FDP is a relatively small group made up of younger white-collar workers and professionals with politically progressive and economically conservative ideals. Since World War II, the FDP has been active in the government by forming coalitions with either the CDU/CSU or the SPD.

ALLIANCE 90/THE GREENS (ALLIANZ 90/ DIE GRÜNEN)

Established in 1979, the Greens won their first *Bundestag* seat in 1983, but lost their seats in 1990 under the five-percent rule. The roots of the party lie in a movement that included various ecology-minded groups, from pacifists to radical factions opposed to nuclear energy. Alliance 90 began in the former East Germany as an offshoot of the civil rights movement that resulted in Germany's reunification. In 1993 the two parties merged, and in 1994 they garnered sufficient votes to be represented in the *Bundestag*.

PARTY OF DEMOCRATIC SOCIALISM (PARTEI DES DEMOKRATISCHEN SOZIALISMUS, PDS)

The newest *Bundestag* party, the PDS evolved from the former Socialist Unity Party, the communist party that ruled East Germany. Its political influence has diminished since the unification of Germany; the PDS holds the fewest seats in Parliament. PDS membership is almost exclusively eastern German, and its main goal is to champion the needs and interests of eastern Germans.

ECONOMY

Germany's economic recovery following World War II was aptly termed the *Wirtschaftswunder* (economic miracle). Germany arose from the devastation of the war to rebuild both its ruined cities and its collapsed economy. Manufacturing began again, and an economic recovery plan drafted by German economist Ludwig Erhard was put into place. This plan included the creation of the Deutsche Bundesbank, Germany's central bank, and the replacement of the Reichsmark with the new Deutsche Mark. Germany was on the road to recovery.

Since that time, Germany has faced minor problems and major crises. Like so many other countries, Germany suffered during the energy crises of the 1970s and rebounded with the economic boom that was the 1980s. Unemployment soared to a high of 8.5% in 1982, inflation to 6.5% in 1981. Since that time, Germany has recovered from the strain of bringing the former East German states up to par with the western states in terms of education, technology, wages, and living standard.

Despite the economic ups and downs of recent years, Germany's economy remains one of the strongest in Europe and is a benchmark for other European Union members.

HOLIDAYS & FESTIVALS

Germany has 11 days that are legal holidays in all states. Three additional dates are legal holidays in some (mainly Catholic) states.

January 1	Neujahrstag	New Year's Day
March/April	Karfreitag	Good Friday
March/April	Ostersonntag	Easter Sunday
March/April	Ostermontag	Easter Monday
May 1	Tag der Arbeit	Labor Day
May/June	Christi Himmelfahrt	Ascension Day
May/June	Pfingstsonntag	Pentecost Sunday
May/June	Pfingstmontag	Pentecost Monday
May/June	Fronleichnamsfest	Corpus Christi*

B A C K G R O U N D

August 15	Mariä Himmelfahrt	Assumption Day*
October 3	Tag der Deutschen Einheit	Day of German Unity
November 1	Allerheiligen	All Saints Day*
December 25	1. Weihnachtstag	Christmas Day
December 26	2. Weihnachtstag	Second Day of Christmas

*Legal holiday only in some states.

In addition to these national days, various states, regions, and cities have their own special celebrations, including music, theater and film, wine, art, and historical festivals. Two events that deserve special mention are *Karneval* and *Oktoberfest*. Christmas and birthdays are also red-letter days on the German cultural calendar.

Karneval (Carnival)

Karneval, also known in the southern regions as *Fasching*, is one of the two periods of sanctioned madness in Germany (the other being *Oktoberfest*, of course). A major event in most Catholic communities, the acknowledged *Karneval* centers are Cologne, Mainz, and Munich. However, even smaller communities invest months of planning in their *Fasching* events. When the time comes, whole cities turn out in fancy dress for parades, parties, and dancing in the streets.

The *Karneval* season (and thus the planning) officially begins at eleven minutes after 11:00 AM on the eleventh day of the eleventh month (St. Martin's Day). The real fun, however, begins in January and culminates in costume balls, parties, and parades during the days immediately preceding Ash Wednesday, which marks the beginning of Lent.

The peak of the *Karneval* events occurs on *Weiberfastnacht* (Women's Fast Night), *Rosenmontag* (Rose Monday), and *Fastnacht* (Night of Fasting). *Weiberfastnacht*, the Thursday before the last weekend of *Karneval*, was originally the only day in which women were allowed to participate in *Karneval*, when they were permitted to "reign" over the city. If you are going to be in Germany on this day, be sure you wear a tie you want to get rid of. One of the traditions of this day is that women are allowed to cut in half the tie of any man they see—and they do.

The big *Karneval* parade is usually held on *Rosenmontag*, with elaborate floats, masked jesters, musicians, and costumed revelers. It can stretch for miles and is traditionally presided over by the *Karneval* "Prince" and "Princess."

Despite its name, *Fastnacht*, the final night of *Karneval*, includes no fasting. Celebrations are held throughout the day, and feature, as usual, eating and drinking. *Karneval* ends at midnight on Shrove Tuesday, and Germans then return to their regular lives. In Munich, this includes the anticipation of *Oktoberfest*.

Oktoberfest

The original *Oktoberfest* was the 1810 celebration of the wedding of Bavarian King Ludwig I to the Saxe-Hildburghausen Princess Therese. Today, *Oktoberfest* is a 16-day festival beginning in late September and ending on the first Sunday in October. It is one of Munich's greatest attractions as well as the largest folk festival in Europe. Gigantic beer tents are erected on a field called the *Theresienwiese* to accommodate the festivities, which consist mainly of drinking beer and eating sausage to the music of oom-pah bands. Traditional costumes (*Lederhosen* and *Dirndls*) abound, especially for the *Trachtenfest* parade featuring more bands, plus floats and decorated beer wagons drawn by draft horses.

Christmas

Christmas is a time reserved primarily for family, and is filled with goodies such as home-baked *Stollen*, *Lebkuchen*, and *Pfeffernüsse*. Many cities have a *Weihnachtsmarkt* (Christmas market) or *Christkindlmarkt* (Christ Child's market); the oldest and most famous is in Nuremberg. These open-air arts and crafts fairs feature handmade Christmas ornaments and the like, *Glühwein* (mulled wine), and other Christmas goodies, such as the cakes and cookies mentioned above.

The Christmas season in Germany is long, but for reasons of tradition, not merely to raise toy sales. The season begins four Sundays before Christmas, at the beginning of Advent. One candle in the *Adventskranz* (Advent wreath) is lit on each of the Sundays leading up to Christmas Day. St. Nikolaustag falls on December 6. St. Nikolaus visits children on the night of December 5; if they've been good, he fills the shoes they have left out with goodies. If the children have been bad, he leaves a bundle of twigs instead. Unlike the jolly man known to American children, St. Nikolaus is a tall, thin old fellow with a long white beard and a long red robe trimmed with white fur.

On *Heiligabend* (Christmas Eve), a bell is rung to signal the family to gather for the unveiling of the Christmas tree, decorated by the *Christkind* (Christ Child) or his earthly deputy, away from the watchful eyes of the family. Christmas presents are distributed, opened, and admired. Christmas midnight Masses are attended by many families. The traditional Christmas Day dinner is goose, although turkey and ham have recently begun to give the goose some competition.

Birthdays

A quick word about birthdays, in case you happen to be in Germany on yours. As the *Geburtstagskind* (birthday boy/girl), it's up to you to arrange the festivities. For children this may mean a party, but adults are by no means exempt. If you're going to the office that day, you are expected to provide some birthday goodies—cake, coffee, perhaps even a bit of the bubbly. You might also like to invite a few close friends for dinner—on you. Expect, too, that friends might drop by your house or apartment to wish you happy birthday, so have a little something ready to serve. As a guest at an office birthday fête, you need only offer a handshake and congratulations, but a small gift is appropriate to give to friends. Don't give a birthday gift in advance, though, since superstition regards that as tempting fate.

EDUCATION

The Educational System

Each of the 16 states is responsible for its own educational system, so there is some difference in the systems from state to state. However, the states work together, and a commission made up of federal and state authorities coordinates the educational policies of the various states. Public education in Germany, even through university and other upper-level schools, is free. While private schools exist, they comprise a small minority of the total.

Kindergarten is available from age 3 to age 6 to supplement learning. Kindergartens, however, are not state schools, so attendance is voluntary and parents must often pay for their children to attend.

German children must attend school from ages 6 to 18, beginning with *Grundschule* (elementary school), which lasts for four years (except in Berlin, where the *Grundschule* is six years). A nice custom for German children comes with a child's first day at school. Children receive a *Schultüte*, a large, gaily decorated cardboard cone overflowing with candy, to celebrate this rite of passage.

Placement by ability and interest begins in the two years following *Grundschule*, known as the *Orientierungsstufe* (orientation stage), when students are expected to make the transition from general learning into a more focused course of study (e.g., science, mathematics, arts, or a vocation). A student's performance during these two crucial years determines the future path of study. Depending on ability and interest, the student enters one of four different types of schools:

The *Gymnasium* is the academic track and includes the *Orientierungsstufe* plus seven more years in the western states and six more years in the eastern states, through grades 13 and 12 respectively. Students at the *Gymnasium* begin with a series of core courses, including mathematics, science, civics, history, German literature and composition, English, and at least one other foreign language. Beginning in the eleventh grade, however, the student concentrates on his or her chosen area of study. The successful completion of *Gymnasium* earns the student a diploma called the *Abitur*, which is the basic requirement for entrance into a university. The course of study at the German *Gymnasium* is more rigorous than at an American high school. Completion of the *Gymnasium* is generally considered the equivalent of the first two years of an American university. Approximately 35% of German students attend *Gymnasium*.

The *Realschule* is the commercial high school, where students receive instruction in both academic and business-related subjects. In addition to core classes, students take courses on the working world. These courses are designed to help them decide on a career path. Students graduate from the *Realschule* with a diploma that will gain them entrance into a business or technical college, or, if their grades are high enough, into the final three years of *Gymnasium*. About 20% of the total German student body attends *Realschule*.

The *Hauptschule*, or general high school, is vocational. Similar to the *Realschule*, its students take core classes, plus courses on their vocational options. Students receive a diploma after the ninth or tenth grade (depending on the state), which allows them to attend formal three-year training programs for technical and clerical professions. These training programs combine vocational training with mandatory classroom instruction at the *Berufschule* (vocational school). The *Hauptschulen* include about 25% of all students.

The *Gesamtschule*, or comprehensive school, is a recent development in Germany, and offers academic, commercial, and vocational programs. Approximately 15% of German children attend *Gesamtschulen*.

Special schools, including those for the physically disabled, account for the remainder of German students.

Following completion of secondary school, various continuing education options exist, depending on one's qualifications. These include *Universitäten* (universities) for *Abitur* holders, *Fachoberschulen* (polytechnic institutes), and *Fachhochschulen* (specialized postgraduate institutions).

Educational Philosophy

The basic ideas of education in Germany differ somewhat from those in the United States. As mentioned above, the track a student will follow is determined at quite an early age, usually around age 11 or 12. Although it is possible for a student to switch from one track to another (from the *Realschule* to *Gymnasium*, for example), it is infrequent and, after a certain point, very difficult, as the subjects offered in the respective schools diverge. In addition, students begin their chosen academic or vocational career path while still in high school, whereas American students generally decide on an academic major after two years of college, or enter the job market with no specialized training after high school.

Grading systems in Germany differ as well. German students' grades are derived mainly from tests, often cumulative tests, rather than from a combination of homework, quizzes, and class participation, as is customary in the United States.

In general, the focus in German schools is on learning, so extracurricular activities are limited. Children who participate in sports and other activities do so in local clubs or community teams rather than in school.

Today, teachers are taught in universities to detect the unique talents of students, and to support and encourage those talents. There is much disagreement about the degree to which discipline should be implemented. The reunification between East and West Germany has not made this problem any easier.

Finally, Germans who are also familiar with the American school system have remarked that the goal of the American system is to encourage the student to discover who he is, while the goal of the German system is to mold students into adults who contribute to society. In America, the student is the sculptor who molds the clay; in Germany, it is the teacher, or educational system, who is the sculptor.

CULTURE

We all have programmed into us a certain code, a set of rules by which we live and interpret the world. These rules govern both our actions and our reactions. They are instilled in us by our parents, our teachers, and our peers. Culture, then, is the combined values, beliefs, mores, motivations, and attitudes that shape our view of the world, or, to use a term borrowed from German, our *Weltanschauung*.

Though we are all individuals, we are influenced by the culture in which we grew up. Despite our individual differences, there are nevertheless cultural ties that bind us together. No matter how little someone from Des Moines seems to have in common with a New Yorker and vice-versa, they are indeed more similar to each other than to people from Tokyo or Riyadh.

This chapter explores the cultural differences between Germany and the United States. Although endless distinctions can be made between cultures, here we break culture down into six different categories that will paint a practical, accessible portrait of German culture viewed through American eyes. These categories are: time, communication, group dynamics, status/hierarchy, relationships, and reasoning style. Each section begins with a brief overview of the category and the polar opposites within it. As we explore the category in more depth, we will take a look at where Germany and the United States fall on the continuum and how they relate to each other. By the end of the section, you should have a greater understanding of what may cause cultural misunderstanding and an idea of the very real challenges communicating across cultures can present. Finally, we will provide you with some tips to help you apply this information to your daily interactions with Germans. We will use this knowledge as we take a step-by-step look at the German business culture in later chapters.

With any luck, you will emerge with a better understanding not only of what makes Germans tick, but of what makes *you* tick as well. Only when you are able to understand that cultural differences are neither bad nor good, merely different ways to look at the same reality, can you begin to build the cross-cultural skills you will need to be successful in Germany—or anywhere else in the world.

The following observations are of necessity painted in broad strokes. It is naturally unwise to think that every German will behave in one way, every American in another. However, there is enough evidence to support the idea that Germans as a culture tend to have certain preferences, as do Americans. Keeping that in mind, the information in this chapter will give you a foundation on which to lay the bricks of individual characteristics and personalities.

TIME

Morgen, morgen, nur nicht heute,
sagen alle faulen Leute.
Tomorrow, tomorrow, not today,
All the lazy people say.

Your company has branches in several European countries. You are in Europe reviewing each branch's progress in designing and implementing a new training program for the sales force and support per-

sonnel. Unfortunately, the visit to each office has to be short, since there are offices in 5 different countries, and you must be back in the States within the week.

Due to your travel schedule, your meeting in Germany is scheduled for 3:00 PM on the last day of your trip. Germany has the largest sales staff of the five offices, and for various reasons it has had difficulty implementing the plan, so there is a considerable amount of information to go over. You dig in, prepared for another long day.

As five o'clock rolls around, your German team members start to fidget and look at their watches, so you call a short break. You notice as you walk down the hall to get another cup of coffee that several people are making phone calls, and you overhear someone saying he will be home late. Good, you think, they are prepared to get this taken care of tonight.

However, by 6:30 it is clear to you that there is a festering resentment running through the meeting. You try to hurry things up, and finally let everyone go at 7:00, although there are still several points that will have to be dealt with by phone and e-mail once you get back to your office.

What the heck just happened, you wonder as you eat yet another late room-service dinner. It seemed like the Germans weren't being team players. Was there some interpersonal problem in the team? Did they resent your leadership of the project? Were they insulted because they were the last ones visited?

Although interpersonal problems are always a possibility whenever two people or more are involved, it is most likely that the problems that arose in the scenario above are the result of different views of time.

Rigid Versus Flexible Cultures

Perhaps the first cultural challenge people encounter, often subconsciously, when they meet another culture is differences in the perception of time. Time is a resource that different cultures view differently. We all have different answers to the questions "What is the value of time?" and "How is time best spent?" In the most basic terms, time can be either flexible or rigid.

In a rigid time culture, the clock is the measure against which all of our actions are judged: whether we are saving time or wasting it, whether we are on time or late. People in rigid time cultures like to plan their activities and keep a schedule. It is rude to show up late and important not to waste other people's time. Time is a commodity that must be spent wisely, not frittered away.

The clock for flexible time cultures is more fluid, and things can happen more spontaneously. Plans are made, but with the understanding that they may be changed, even at the last minute, depending on circumstances. Punctuality is not a virtue, and many things can take precedence over adherence to a schedule.

German-American Interaction

While Germans and Americans both fall on the rigid end of the time spectrum, there are nevertheless significant differences between the two cultures. Germans have the reputation of being one of the most, if not the most, time-conscious cultures in the world, and deservedly so. Anyone trying to get by day-to-day in Germany has to become very aware of time. Indeed, certain things can only be done at certain times. Shopping is dictated by early shop closings, your window of opportunity for washing your car is dictated by law, and quiet times are strictly imposed. This carries over into the business world as well, where you are expected to be on time for appointments and most people leave work at the stroke of 5:00. While you will find a train arriving late now and then, and some Germans are late to meetings, the general perception of Germans as very time-conscious people remains accurate.

While Americans certainly fall on the rigid end of the time spectrum, they fall short of the Germans. Americans do like their schedules, but schedules are more flexible in the sense that last-minute appointments and cancellations are accepted, behavior which strikes most Germans as irresponsible. American businesspeople, especially those in management positions, are expected to meet deadlines and finish projects, even if it means staying until the wee hours of the morning. A German, on the other hand, wouldn't feel the least bit guilty taking a day off, even if a project isn't done, as long as he worked hard on it. For Germans, there is a time for everything.

Whereas the German time-consciousness revolves around planning, American time-consciousness is all about speed. When Germans and Americans work in the same office, the Germans often feel that the Americans waste a lot of time "at the coffee machine"; that is, they spend too much time chatting with their co-workers instead of doing their jobs. If Americans were only more efficient, think the Germans, they wouldn't have to stay until seven every night just to get their jobs done. Americans, on the other hand, are astonished when the Germans pick up and leave promptly at 5:00. This, they think, must mean that the Germans don't have the same amount of dedication to their jobs.

More on Time

- Be on time! This applies to both business appointments and social occasions. One American living in Germany swears that her German guests arrive 10 minutes early, then drive or walk around the block until they can ring her doorbell at exactly the appointed time.
- Try to plan ahead as much as possible. You will have to do a certain amount of planning around the open hours of stores, banks, and other places.
- Remember that as a rule most Germans prefer that you make arrangements to meet, rather than just dropping by their desks or homes without warning.

COMMUNICATION

Lügen haben kurze Beine.
Lies have short legs.

After 6 months in Germany, Pamela Monroe was growing more and more frustrated with her job as HR manager. She was frankly astonished by the way the department was run. The HR department seemed to have no formal system for evaluating employees. She had proposed the idea of setting up such a system, and even volunteered to take the lead on the project. Her idea consisted of both a peer evaluation and an evaluation by the immediate supervisor. But the resistance she met was stronger than the proverbial brick wall.

What was worse than that, though, was her own predicament. She was growing increasingly unsure and—dare she admit it?—paranoid about her position in the company. Although she felt that she was doing a good job, she was unable to get any feedback on her performance. Whenever she asked anyone for informal feedback, they just said that there were no problems. "Alles gut," perhaps, but she sure didn't feel that way.

Direct Versus Indirect Communication

What is the goal of communication? Regardless of what culture you are from, you need to be able to relay information to other people. But is that the goal in and of itself, or are there other variables that affect the goal?

In cultures that value direct communication, the goal of communication is mainly to relay information. Value is placed on being able to state your point in a clear and concise manner, and words have limited nuances. In general, people do not appreciate having to pull the real point out of a surfeit of words.

If you live in a culture of indirect communication, on the other hand, you have to take other factors into account. It may be important not to cause offense to your listener, to show deference, or to maintain harmony, for example. Very often the real meaning in indirect communication cultures is a subtext buried under many layers or intertwined with non-verbal clues or metaphor.

German-American Interaction

Americans have many sayings about speaking directly. "Don't beat around the bush." "Just spit it out." "Get to the point." Their German counterparts feel the same way, but they favor a more universal application of those maxims. One of the most common miscommunications that happen between Americans and Germans is in the use of niceties, not only in social situations, but in business as well. American workers are used to hearing "Could you do this?," "I need you to do this," and even "Would you mind doing that?" "Please" and "thank you" are standards of the American business vocabulary. Germans have more of an implicit understanding of what one's duties are; therefore, it is not necessary for a boss to couch a directive as a request.

An American giving a performance review will start first with some positive comments: improvements that the employee has made, goals achieved, etc. This affirmation of the employee's contributions is followed by "constructive criticism," wherein the manager discusses goals not achieved, slippage in performance, and so on. Even here the language is somewhat indirect, and directives for improvement are stated as suggestions for improvement. A German performance review—if there is one—will focus more on the improvements needed than the successes of the past year. Affirmation is not necessary, since it is expected that each person do his or her job. No news is assumed to be good news. When the two styles meet you get either a German who feels wrapped in cotton, somewhat dazed by the back-and-forth of compliment and criticism, or an American who feels personally assaulted and frustrated that his or her contributions weren't appreciated or even acknowledged.

More on Communication

- Develop a thick skin! Remind yourself not to take it personally when you encounter the more direct style of speaking that is typical in Germany.
- Try to speak honestly and frankly. But don't confuse a direct communication style with rudeness. There is a difference between being frank and being tactless.
- Americans are notorious for tossing around casual compliments. This is usually a mechanism meant to demonstrate an interest in the other person. However, in Germany, excessive compliments will earn you the reputation of being insincere. Do you really love every single blouse and scarf your co-worker wears? Conversely, if you should get a compliment from a German boss or co-worker, you should view it as a sincere appreciation.

GROUP DYNAMICS

When he first arrived in Germany, Keith Armstrong had been favorably impressed by the way his German co-workers worked independently. His staff required little instruction and he could generally

count on things being done efficiently. He was quite surprised, there-
fore, by the dynamics at his team's first strategy meeting. The discus-
sion of the potential paths was quite lengthy and very detailed. The
Germans seemed intent on examining each and every potential out-
come under a microscope. Finally, Keith had had enough. He sug-
gested that the group simply agree to disagree and take a vote to find
out which pieces of the puzzle the majority of the group could agree
on. To his surprise, the German team members objected. They seemed
determined to work out a plan that would satisfy each and every per-
son. Given their independent approach to their jobs, this sudden con-
cern for consensus baffled Keith.

Group-Oriented Versus Individualistic

In the overall scheme of things, which is stronger: the needs of the
individual or the needs of the group? Is it usually the case that indi-

viduals are willing to make sacrifices for the good of the group, or will the group suffer for the benefit of the individual?

We are all faced at one time or another with making a decision to place someone else's needs before our own—our family, our friends, our team at work. Where the deeper cultural differences lie, however, is in the expectations of society. What is the societal norm for looking out for oneself or one's group? The next time you stay late at the office, think about your motives for doing so. Are you really staying to finish the project because it will be an enormous benefit to your company? Or are you staying because in order to advance up the ladder of success it is important that you be perceived as dedicated and hard-working?

Groups can take on many forms. Your group might consist of your family (immediate or extended), co-workers, the company you work for, friends with whom you grew up and went to school, a tribe or clan, a religious group, or a local, regional, or national affiliation. And of course you may belong to many different groups throughout your life.

If you are group-oriented, the group is an inherent part of your identity. You are first and foremost Japanese or Muslim or Bantu or a member of the Fuentes family, and a major factor in your decisions and actions is how they affect other members of your group. As an individual you are much more inclined to align your own goals with those of the group. Your talent is part of a larger pool, and when you cooperate with others it becomes possible to reach a mutual goal.

For example, some of the sales people in your division may bring in more revenue and some less. However, the important thing is that the sales goals be met, so everyone should share equally in the annual bonus. In this way, individual weaknesses are compensated for by others' strengths so that a balance is achieved. The success of the team strengthens it as a group and encourages people to strive for higher goals.

The sales scenario wherein everyone shares equally in the bonus when some people bring in more business than others seems unfair in individualistic cultures. Sure, it's great to meet sales goals, one may think, but since I was responsible for more revenue than the other members of the team, I should receive a larger share of the annual bonus. In this mindset, if everyone gets an equal share of the bonus, people are tempted to coast along and not put maximum effort into their jobs. In an individualistic culture, it is important that everyone receive the recognition due him or her and, conversely, that everyone take responsibility for his or her mistakes.

A culture's inclination toward the group or the individual will be an important influence in areas such as teamwork, rewards and motivation, and decision-making.

German-American Interaction

Americans pride themselves on their individualism. They like to be different, to stand out in a crowd. They are ingrained with the notion that each person should be responsible for his own actions. From infancy, American children are encouraged to make their own choices. When they grow up, many move far away from home. This mobility does not create an environment in which closely-knit extended families or groups of friends can survive. Instead, it fosters a strong sense of individuality.

Germans, while largely individualistic, especially in comparison to many other countries, have some elements of group orientation. Although people are responsible for their own actions, they also have some responsibility to society, to their neighbors. As mentioned in the section on time above, a German who wants to crank up his stereo will have to bow to the wishes of his neighbors who have expressed a desire for a designated quiet time. And unlike Americans, Germans tend to stick close to home, a habit that allows for the continuation of familial and school relationships.

Keeping in mind that this is a hypothetical generalization, the following illustration may be helpful in summarizing. An American child who is coloring a picture can color the sky purple or green if she so desires. A German child might be told that since the sky is blue, she must color it blue. You might say, then, that Germans allow themselves individual expression within the confines of societal norms.

More on Individualism

- Remember that your "rights" as an individual do not override those of the people around you. Everyone is bound by the obligation to respect the rules that allow everyone to co-exist in relative peace and harmony.

STATUS & HIERARCHY

Janice Miller needed to place an order with her supplier, a German company. She called in the order, but her account representative didn't answer the phone. Janice left a message with the receptionist and, just to make sure the account rep got the message, shot off an e-mail as well. When she didn't hear back from the account rep by the end of the following day, Janice began to get impatient. She needed the shipment to meet her deadline, and she certainly didn't have time to spend trying to get in touch with the account rep. So Janice placed another call, this time to the regional sales manager. She explained that she had not been able to get in touch with her account rep, and asked the sales manager to take care of the order for her. She got the order, but the next time she called to talk to her usual account rep, she could almost feel the icy blast of arctic air coming from the telephone. What's going on, she thought? What kind of customer service is this?

Ascribed Versus Achieved Status

Social strata are inherent in all cultures. How we differ is in the way that we gain and attribute status. Do we acquire status by virtue of who we are or by what we do?

Status can be based on the inherent characteristics of a person, over which we have no control, such as age, race, gender, or family background. Or it may be based on what a person has accomplished, including educational and professional qualifications, such as the school one attended or whether one is a sign painter or a doctor.

Certainly when we evaluate other people we use a mixture of these criteria. However, a culture will generally value one over the other. In an ascribed status culture, for example, an employee must show competence in order to advance in his or her job; however, he or she must also have seniority. The wisdom and experience that come with age are valued. Similarly, a manager might be influenced in his or her hiring decisions by the applicant's family background or social connections—or lack thereof. Social strata are generally well defined and one does not easily move between them.

It is much more common in achieved status cultures to accord status based on accomplishments. Social strata are less defined and it is not uncommon to move up the social ladder. While there are certain benefits that come with seniority, it is certainly possible for younger employees to be promoted above their elders. A person's past and, perhaps more importantly, future performance is valued above age. Many U.S. companies, in fact, have a certain number of "fast track" employees who are expected to move up quickly through the ranks based on their potential performance.

Vertical Versus Lateral Hierarchy

Another aspect of status is whether the hierarchical structure is vertical or lateral. It's important to remember that hierarchy exists in all cultures, whether it is overt or hidden.

In a vertical hierarchy, the structure tends to be overt. Positions within the hierarchy, corporate or social, are clearly outlined, and it is expected that people show and receive the respect due to them as a result of their position within the hierarchy. This respect is shown in many ways, from the use of titles to the depth of one's bow to the vocabulary one uses. The expatriate manager who tries to get his subordinates to call him "Dave" in a vertical hierarchy probably isn't going to have much luck—his employees will feel uncomfortable using such a disrespectfully familiar form of address to their boss. The title "Mr. Dave" may be the closest his subordinates come to using his first name.

Lateral hierarchies allow more equality among colleagues. Each person must be respected for his or her ability, regardless of position in the company. The more egalitarian nature of lateral hierarchies usually means a more informal environment. Lateral hierarchies also allow for greater empowerment at lower levels, as most decisions related to their jobs are made by employees themselves, with less direct instruction from superiors. There is less concern for following the exact lines of authority than there is for finding the person who is in a position to take care of the issue at hand. Therefore, an employee who needs information from someone in another part of the business would have the freedom to approach that person directly, rather than channeling the request up through his boss, then on to the other person's boss, and finally down to the person who has the information, a restriction that an employee in a hierarchical organization would find difficult to circumvent.

You will find that a culture's views of the nature and importance of status influences business in the relationship and interaction between superiors and subordinates, in the way that information flows (or does not flow) between individuals, in the decision-making process, and in how people move up through the ranks, to name but a few issues.

German-American Interaction

By global standards, both Germany and the United States fall toward the achieved status side of the pendulum, but both Germans and Americans are a mixed bag of values, sometimes even contradicting themselves. Germans tend to have a more vertical hierarchy, Americans a more lateral hierarchy.

One indicator of a vertical hierarchy is the use of more formality and titles, most assuredly a German trait, while the situation in the United States is quite the opposite. Germans also have in place lines of authority that must be followed without fail, whereas Americans don't mind jumping over people in the line of authority if it is necessary to get the job done.

However, there are fewer levels of organizational status in Germany than in the United States. For example, the difference between the salary of the highest-paid employee and the lowest-paid employee in a German organization will be much smaller than in the United States; most German executives simply do not get salaries in the millions. And whereas most Americans expect to be promoted quickly regardless of their age, it is not as common in Germany to see young people in positions of authority.

That said, it must be noted that the traditional vertical structure of German companies is a legacy of their past. While this structure remains in most of the older companies, some of which have been around for over a century, newer, younger companies are moving to a much flatter hierarchy as a new generation comes into its own with its own ideas.

Generally speaking, German society does not have as many layers as American society, but movement between strata in the United States is easier than in Germany.

More on Status & Hierarchy

- Most Germans are not overly concerned with social hierarchy. The car one drives is a better indicator of social status than the clothes one wears or where one went to school.
- In the business environment, it is important to respect the company's hierarchy and work within it.
- Many positions that are considered inferior in the United States, such as secretary or skilled laborer, require extensive training in Germany (mostly a minimum of 3 years). Be careful to treat people in these positions as professionals.

RELATIONSHIPS

Monica Perez had been in Germany for four months, and she had finally reached the conclusion that her German co-workers would never warm up to her. She had done her best to get to know them, but no one seemed interested. At first Monica had tried asking people about their weekends on Monday morning, but she had received such

noncommittal answers that she had soon abandoned that tactic. Time after time, her colleagues had skirted her attempts to get to know them. Monica had always thought of herself as a congenial person who made friends easily, so she was baffled to find that none of the people at work wanted to be friends.

Relationship-Oriented Versus Task-Oriented

In the business of life, what takes the priority: your personal relationships or the tasks you do? If you are from a relationship-oriented culture, relationships come before tasks, and, in fact, may be necessary in order to perform tasks. This can have many implications. A sickness in the family (even the extended family) may take precedence over work; a chance meeting with a friend might delay a scheduled meeting; a deal might not be struck until both parties have had time to build a basis of mutual respect and trust. Relationships—ones that go beyond just working together—are the cornerstones of a life of interdependent networks and are a goal in and of themselves.

Task-oriented folks, on the other hand, tend to focus on the job at hand and leave the relationships to whatever time is left over after the work is finished. No friendship or personal intimacy is necessary to perform one's job and it is generally considered more professional not to let one's personal life intrude on one's work. The general rule is that one should get on with one's business and worry about "being friends" later.

This is not to say that relationship-builders don't get things done; nor is it meant to imply that task-focused people are not friendly. It simply means that the expectations one has in one's personal and business relationships might not be the same as what is expected in another culture. If you are doing business abroad, you will find that these differences can be crucial to your success. You will see them crop up in negotiating, making deals, getting information, making sales, joint ventures, and team building, to name but a few areas.

Rule Abiding Versus Rule Bending

A subset of the relationship-versus-task puzzle is the issue of relationships vis-à-vis rules. Should rules (this includes both actual laws
and the unwritten rules of society) have a universal application, or is
there room to maneuver—or even circumvent them?

Germany is a country with a strong belief in the universal application of rules. This applies equally to crossing the street (law) and
the ordering protocol at the butcher shop (rule). If you are a pedestrian stopped at a "Don't Walk" signal, you stand on the corner until
the light changes to "Walk," even if there is no traffic in sight. As you
enter the shop, you determine where you are in the imaginary line
(there probably is no real queue), and wait until it is your turn to
place your order. What's more, you will be told if you are breaking
the rules, by passersby, by fellow motorists, by your neighbors. In
Germany it is generally safe to assume that there is a protocol and a
rule for almost everything; it behooves you to find out what those
rules are and adhere to them. Some of the more common "rules and
regulations" can be found in the Living and Staying in Germany and
Business Step-by-Step sections.

German-American Interaction

Here again, the United States and Germany are on the same side of
the coin as task-oriented cultures. But one important way that
Americans and Germans do differ is in the relationship between
one's personal and professional lives.

Americans find it easy to blend their two lives. Co-workers will
discuss their personal lives at work—their families, activities, and
even romantic relationships—and vice versa. A typical topic of conversation at an American party is one's job. Americans often further
the mingling of their work and personal lives by socializing with
their co-workers outside of the business environment.

Germans prefer to keep their personal and private lives separate. It is inappropriate to discuss personal issues in the workplace, and equally inappropriate to talk about your work at a social gathering. The relative lack of mobility among Germans usually means that friendships begun in school last a lifetime. This established social network that is already in place when one enters the work force allows Germans to neatly compartmentalize their private and work lives.

Perhaps even more important are the differences in the way that Germans and Americans build relationships. Americans are friendly people, and it's usually easy to meet people in the United States. Germans tend to be more reserved and distant. However, after a time, a German will find that a friendship with an American will only go so deep. Germans often feel that Americans come on strong, but there is no real substance to a friendship; it's more what they would call an acquaintanceship. Americans, of course, complain that Germans are hard to get to know. It's harder to make social contacts (remember, Germans already have a circle of friends), and it takes people longer to warm up to one another.

More on Relationships

- Don't expect to make friends overnight. Most Americans find that it takes longer to build friendships in Germany.
- Don't necessarily expect to become friends with your co-workers.
- Respect the separation of business and private lives.
- Joining one of the many clubs for any type of leisure activity is a good way to meet people in a non-work environment.

REASONING

Jeff Montgomery was well prepared for his presentation to the German subsidiary of his company. During his brief visit to

Germany, Jeff was charged with presenting the company's marketing plan for its newest product. His presentation clearly outlined the goals of the market strategy and the way that they would arrive at those goals. Jeff was well into his presentation when he was interrupted by an audience member who inquired about the steps that had led the company to decide on the goals of the marketing scheme. Jeff hadn't planned on presenting that particular information, but he nevertheless gave a brief overview of how the decision had been made. Several other members of the audience piped up with questions about that topic as well. Jeff eventually managed to get back to his planned presentation, only to find himself again sidetracked by requests from the audience for details that were outside the scope of his presentation. What was meant to be a half-hour presentation had turned into a question-and-answer session that Jeff had not anticipated. After an hour he began to wonder if he should continue to allow these tangential questions or if he should force the presentation back onto its original track.

Pragmatic, Analytical, or Holistic Reasoning

Perhaps the most complex manifestation of culture is found in our thought processes. Around the world, the way people reason can be divided into three general styles: pragmatic, analytical, or holistic.

Pragmatic thinkers begin with the goal and seek the steps that will enable them to attain that goal. The emphasis is therefore on finding practical ways to solve a problem or reach a goal. For example, if the goal is to increase sales by 10% in a given year, the task is then to identify the means of doing so. A pragmatic thinker will, for example, compile information on increasing his or her client base and on the purchases made by current clients. The pragmatic thinker's final report might include a brief mention of all of the ideas presented, but its most prominent point will be the recommendation of certain sales strategies and how best to implement these strategies.

Analytical thinkers take the reverse approach, focusing on the process with the goal as the logical conclusion. So an analytical thinker's approach to the problem of increasing sales by 10% will be different. He or she will begin by exploring all options, including increasing client base and increasing purchases. From there the analytical thinker will select the strategies that will be the most beneficial, leading to the conclusion that it is possible to increase sales by 10% in a given year. This increase then becomes the goal.

Holistic thinkers incorporate both of the methods above, but they also tend to include elements in their thinking that most pragmatic and analytical thinkers would not. In determining sales, a holistic thinker would examine the information gathered on the potential and current client base, but he or she might also add a few things to the mix. For example, a holistic thinker may ask, what are the possibilities of expanding the current range of products? Even if the pragmatic and analytical thinkers above had thought of this scenario, it is much more likely to be in a linear fashion. That is, a seller of office products who is not a holistic thinker would not get into selling, say, women's lingerie. Holistic thinkers tend to be more non-linear in their thinking and may see a relationship between office products and women's lingerie that pragmatic and analytical thinkers do not, such as the fact that they have a ready supplier of both. Another example of a potential question asked by a holistic thinker is what the impact may be on the sales staff. Will the higher quotas require them to work more hours in the week or spend more time away from their families? Finally, after putting all of the pieces in to the puzzle, the holistic thinker will see that it is possible to increase sales by 10%.

As you can see, each of the three scenarios above ended up in the same place: a 10% increase in sales. However, the road taken in each instance traveled through different terrain, even different countries. This difference in reasoning styles has an unmistakable impact on doing business abroad. Its significance is readily apparent in the process of decision-making, in writing reports and making presentations, and even in communicating.

German-American Interaction

This category offers the clearest example of cultural differences between Germany and the United States. Americans are some of the world's most pragmatic thinkers. That is to say, Americans focus on the bottom line, a favorite phrase. Background information need not be extensively reviewed, since implementing a strategy to reach a goal is most important. Germans, though, are some of the world's greatest analytical thinkers. Review of background information is key to understanding the goals, and from there, the strategy.

Tell an American that the ice-cream store has decided to add a new flavor and he will start working on how to market it. Tell a German that the ice-cream store has decided to add a new flavor and he will want to know how the decision was reached—what research methods were used, what other flavors were tested, what the ingredients of the new flavor will be. The American will eventually inquire about some of the details of the product research, and the German will begin working on the marketing plan once he has digested the background information. If they are working together,

they will eventually arrive at a mutually agreeable marketing strategy and implementation plan, but not without some frustration on
the part of both.

Generally speaking, Germans require a lot more detail than
Americans and would prefer to have the whole picture rather than
just the end result. Germans working with Americans often find
them impatient and interested only in "the point," while the
Americans find their German counterparts to be overly concerned
with details.

More on Reasoning

- In business, be prepared with a lot of background information.
- Try to approach your business tasks, such as presentations and
  reports, with an analytical mindset, starting at the beginning
  and covering details rather than summarizing.
- Expect that German colleagues will ask questions to fill in gaps
  in the background and in details if you don't provide them.

WHAT DOES IT ALL MEAN?

As you have probably already noticed, there are often correlations
among the above categories. None of the six categories exists in a
vacuum. If relationships are more important to you, it follows that
you will be more willing to spend time (or waste it, from a task-oriented point of view) getting to know people before plunging into the
task; relationship-oriented cultures tend to also be flexible time cultures. Similarly, if strong and harmonious relationships are your
goal, that will be reflected in the way you communicate; relationship-
oriented cultures also tend to be indirect communication cultures.
You see the pattern.

Compared to the rest of the world, Germans and Americans
have a lot in common. Just as the Iowan at the beginning of the section found some similarities with New Yorkers when compared to
natives of Tokyo, so too do Americans and Germans find themselves

falling on the same end of the spectrum in many of the cultural categories. The key to German-American interaction, then, is understanding the nuances of difference: How much more time-conscious are Germans? What are their thought processes? And so on.

In a sense, it can be more difficult for an American to adapt to the cultural differences in Germany than in Japan or Mexico. Because the cultural differences between the United States and Asia or Latin America are so blatant, and even vast, we are expecting the challenges. However, we often have an inherent expectation that European countries are just like us, except for the fact that they speak other languages. So we can be sideswiped when we do encounter the cultural differences; the fact that they are often subtle differences, noted by our subconscious more often than not, makes it more difficult to understand where the problems lie and how to adapt effectively.

That's the bad news; the good news is that with knowledge, practice and, most of all, respect for the German culture, it can be done. Chapters 6 and 7 will outline the differences in business cultures between the United States and Germany and give you some practical advice on living and doing business in Germany.

THREE

LIVING ABROAD:
Thoughts Before You Go

Most people face an international move with a combination of excitement and apprehension. Moving within the confines of your home country can be difficult enough; moving across borders adds a whole new dimension of cultural differences which can magnify the stress we all naturally feel in a new environment.

The single most important thing that you can do to ensure a successful sojourn abroad is to have realistic expectations. Unfortunately, it's difficult to gauge how realistic your expectations are before you go. You can, however, help define your perspective by considering the following points.

- **What do you hope to get out of your stay abroad?** If you will be working while you're abroad, your company will have certain expectations about the goals of your job, but it is up to you to set your own goals for personal and professional development. Be specific. Although "broadening my horizons" is an admirable goal, "gaining an understanding of the domestic automotive market" is a marketable skill that you will be able to use. If you will not be employed, it is essential that you make plans now for how you will occupy your time in the new country. What skills and interests do you have that you can apply to your advantage? You will have many options, including volunteering, continuing your education, or developing a hobby or skill into a freelance business.

- **If you have a partner and/or children, are you starting out with a sound relationship with your partner and with your children?** Although it may be tempting to regard an international assignment as a time to make a fresh start, it is not advisable to use the assignment to try to mend a troubled relationship. An inherent problem with living abroad is the stress caused by being in a new environment and the additional stress of confronting a foreign language and culture. A marriage or partnership that is in trouble, or a family with strained relationships, is more likely to crumble with the added pressure. Couples and families who start out with healthy relationships often find that their ties are strengthened by an international assignment. Each person is able to offer the support and encouragement necessary to create a positive environment with open lines of communication.

- **How much do you know about daily life in the country you are moving to?** It's one thing to know about the history of a country, to be familiar with the cultural icons and know where the best hotels are. But how much do you know about the infrastructure of the country? How much does it cost to live there? What is it like to go shopping? What is the definition of "service" in that country? Will you be able to find babysitters, go to a nightclub alone, wear shorts, ski? In other words, will you be able to find all of the things that you count on to make your life easier and more pleasurable? And if you can't, can you live without them or find acceptable substitutes? These are very important questions to answer *before* you go. Most of the information is not difficult to find if you are willing to look for it. You can use the Internet, find books, or talk to people who have lived there.

Of course, you may not be planning this relocation alone, and, if not, there's a good deal to consider regarding your children and your partner. We'll start with the children.

IMPACT ON CHILDREN

Accepting an international assignment is a decision that affects everyone in your family, including children. Kids react in a variety of ways, with excitement, resentment, and fear. Children can benefit enormously from living internationally. They will develop the ability to look at the world multi-dimensionally and to interact successfully with a wide variety of people; they will also tend to be open-minded and less judgmental. Unfortunately, at the beginning of an assignment, those benefits are on a distant horizon. What you have to deal with immediately is getting your children acclimated to their new lives as painlessly as possible.

Any kind of move can be difficult for children; being uprooted from friends and school and getting adjusted to a strange place is not easy. With an international move, along with the usual questions of "Will anyone like me?" and "Will I be able to make friends?", children have to deal with a new culture, where kids may look different, talk differently, or act differently—or all of the above. Fortunately, there are many steps you can take to smooth the transition.

First of all, involve children in the decision to move abroad.

That is not to say that you must allow your child the chance to veto the move. The first reaction of most children to any move—domestic or international—is generally negative. (In fact, if a child reacts positively, it may be a sign of an underlying problem. Your child may be viewing the move as an escape hatch.) But you can let your child know as early as possible about the move. Take the time to discuss why the move is necessary. This is especially important for older children and teens. They are old enough to be involved in discussions about why this move will help mom's or dad's career.

Secondly, let your child express all of his or her feelings about the move. A child's emotions will probably run the gamut from anger to excitement at one time or another. Share your own feelings, too. Let your child know that it's a little scary for you, too, but also exciting. Most importantly, let your child know that it's okay to feel anxious, excited, scared, or angry.

Another important way to help children adjust is to talk about expectations. Be optimistic, but prepare to accept the bad as well as the good. Don't hide the fact that it is going to be hard at times, but don't forget to emphasize the positive. Help your kids learn about their destination. Make it a family project in which you all participate. The more realistic your child's expectations are—and your own too, incidentally—the easier the transition will be.

An easy way to ease a transition abroad is to take items from the house and from your child's room that will make the new house or apartment feel like home. Continuity is a key factor in a child's adjustment. Even though it may be tempting to leave a lot of items and replace them when you get to your destination, try to take as many of your children's belongings as possible. It is worth the trouble of packing and shipping if your child's bicycle or her own familiar bed help her to become comfortable with her new home.

Just as you involved your children in the decision to move, involve children in the actual move as much as possible. Children feel helpless during an international move. They are being moved abroad without having much say in the matter. It will help lessen the feelings of helplessness if you let children make as many decisions as you can. Let your child choose favorite toys or furniture, a favorite picture from the living room, or other items that you will take with you.

Allow your children the opportunity to say goodbye to their friends. Have a party and let the children invite their friends, or enlist the help of a teacher in throwing a class party. Take videos or lots of pictures to make an album to bring with you. Adults are sometimes surprised that young children have as deep an attachment to their playmates and possessions as older children. With all children, it is important to recognize the sense of loss and grieving that children go through when moving. Making "good good-byes" is an important step in being ready to accept the new.

Finally, make plans for staying in touch with family and friends. Make an address book for younger children to write the addresses of their friends in so that they can write. Think about other ways to stay in touch, such as a round-robin newsletter, faxing, e-mailing, or creating an audio- or videotape that you can send home. Create a schedule for a weekly or monthly telephone call, writing letters, or making your tapes.

There is no formula that you can use to determine how your child is going to react. And obviously two children in the same family can have totally opposite reactions, with one skipping cheerfully off to school right away and one suffering stomachaches that double him over in pain. Personality plays a part in the adjustment, but so do the parents and the environment created in the new home. Following are some descriptions of general behavior patterns. As you read these descriptions, consider how your child has reacted to stressful situations in the past—this will give you insight into how he might react to an international move, which is most assuredly stressful—and give some thought to how you can help him manage his cultural transition.

By the Way...

EENIE, MEENIE, MINEY, MOE...

Want to give your kids an edge? Teach them this counting rhyme, handy for choosing who's "it," selecting the right cookie, and so much more...

Zicke, zacke, zecke,
Zecke, zicke, zacke,
Zi, za, zaus,
Du bist 'raus!

And as a bonus, here's a tongue twister. See if you can get your tongue around it. It means "Black cats scratch with black claws," but it's much more fun in German.

Schwarze Katzen kratzen mit schwarzen Tatzen.

Infants and Toddlers

While the biggest disruption for infants is the change in sleeping and eating schedules, toddlers will have a harder time understanding what is happening, and will require a great deal of reassurance, before, during, and after the move. Distress at this age often results in a regression to babyish, clinging behavior.

Preschoolers

Preschool-aged children should be involved in the move as much as possible. Create ways that they can help, such as selecting which toys and clothing to bring and which to leave, labeling the boxes from his or her room, and packing for the trip. Seeing things being put into boxes and knowing that they will be unpacked in a few weeks is reassuring. Games will help explain the move; you can stage a play move with a doll house or by packing up and "moving" in your child's wagon. Coloring and activity books and picture books of your destination will add to the sense of security. Don't forget that shipped boxes may take several weeks to arrive. Make sure you take some of your familiar items on the plane with you.

Preteens

Older children will have more questions and will require more explanations. Take the time to discuss why you are moving, and be open about your feelings about moving. It helps children to know that their parents are sad to be leaving behind the people they know but are looking forward to a new experience. Learn with your children about your new country. Make trips to the library and select books that you can read together. Get a world map and a map of the country so they can see where they are going. Work with your children's teachers to make a presentation about the country. Learn about the food, traditional clothing, or holidays of the country. You can also help your children learn some phrases in the new language. Make a game of learning how to say "please" and "thank you" and other simple phrases. And give older children as much responsibility as possible in getting ready to move.

Teens

Teenagers often have the most difficulty with a major move. They are at a time in their lives when they are trying to establish an identity separate from their families and gain independence. The identity being shaped is linked to friends and social activities; changes make things all the more difficult. Moving to another country adds more pressure in the form of a potential language barrier and unknown customs. The best way to help teenagers through this period is through open communication. Let them know that what they are feeling is okay. You can also help by finding out as much information as possible about where you are going. Get information on the new school, including the curriculum and extracurricular activities.

Finding out how kids dress and what they like to do when they get together is important too.

Although living abroad is a rewarding experience, some circumstances make it preferable to allow a teenager to remain behind for the remainder of a semester or a school year (especially in the case of high-school seniors). Include your teenager in the discussion and make the decision based on the needs of your family.

All children, no matter what age, pick up on and, to a certain extent, reflect the behavior of their parents. Therefore, a positive attitude on your part is the best way to influence your children. Your enthusiasm and acceptance of your new life will help them adjust; the way you handle your own frustrations will set the example for them.

IMPACT ON SPOUSES OR PARTNERS

In the majority of cases, expatriates who accompany their spouse or partner abroad are not able to get the necessary permit to work in the host country. If you are giving up or postponing a career or job to make this move with your partner, you are suddenly faced with a great deal of free time that you will have to occupy in the new country.

Giving Up or Postponing a Career

At first glance, having several months—or even several years—of free time may sound like a dream come true. In fact, there are probably few people who wouldn't welcome an extended vacation. However, you will find that after a couple of weeks of inactivity you will begin to feel restless. For most people, a career provides a lot of their self-identity and feeling of self-worth, and its absence will certainly leave a void.

Being a Stay-at-Home Parent

When there are children in the family, the accompanying partner often decides to give up his or her career with the expectation that staying at home with the kids will provide more than enough to do. Before making this decision, here are a couple of issues to consider.

- How old are your children?
- Will your children be attending school?
- If your children will be in school, how do you plan to occupy your time when they are gone?
- Are there ways to get involved with your children's activities (i.e., volunteering at the school, coaching, leading field trips, etc.)?

DUELING CAREERS

The most pressing concern for dual-career couples is usually finding a position for the accompanying partner. It is important to stress that while it is not always possible to find a paid position, there are usually plenty of other opportunities. The best way to find a "job" while you are living abroad is to redefine what "work" is. Broaden your definition from a nine-to-five job to include a host of other things, such as volunteering (which may lead to a paid position), freelancing, consulting, continuing your education, or learning new skills.

The following questions will help you begin to plan for identifying an occupation while you are abroad.

- Is it possible to get the permit you need to be eligible to work in that country? Can your company or your partner's company help you obtain one?
- Are there any opportunities within your company in the new location (either in a local office, if there is one, or as a consultant or working on a project for your company that can be accomplished from abroad)?
- Are there any similar opportunities within your partner's company?
- Are there entrepreneurial possibilities that you can pursue while abroad?
- Does either your company or your partner's company offer any

type of career counseling or job location assistance that would help you find a suitable position abroad? (This can sometimes be negotiated as part of the relocation package.)

- Are there volunteer opportunities in your field that you would consider appropriate substitutes for a paid position?
- Are there other opportunities outside of your field that you would consider appropriate substitutes for a paid position?
- Do you have a hobby or other interest that you could capitalize on? For example, if you have an interest in photography, can you freelance or assist a professional photographer?
- Is this an opportunity to make a career change? You will have a period of time that you can put to use learning new skills or developing your skills in a different direction.
- Keep in mind that even freelance work may require a work permit unless you are working solely for U.S. clients.
- Do you speak the local language well enough to consider opportunities outside of English-speaking organizations?

So far in this section we've taken a look at some important points to remember when considering the impact of a move abroad on yourself, your children, and your partner. Another major issue is cultural adaptation, or, in other words, what you should expect as you look ahead at your and your family's acclimation to a new culture.

UNDERSTANDING CULTURAL ADAPTATION

Culture shock, or cultural disorientation, is the result of finding yourself in a culture that is new and unfamiliar. People in the new culture not only speak a different language, they also live by a different set of rules, with different values, attitudes, and behaviors. In some cases, these differences are immediately obvious; in others they are quite subtle. Cultural disorientation results in a range of emotional reactions, from irritation and frustration to anxiety and

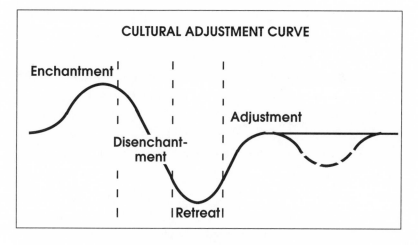

insecurity to resentment and anger. If the cultural adaptation process is not well managed, it will lead to depression.

No one is immune to culture shock; even frequent travelers and people who have lived abroad before feel its effect. The exception to the rule is the person who experiences mild culture shock in an abbreviated form. For the vast majority of us, though, culture shock has a significant impact. The key to managing the cultural adaptation process is understanding what it is and developing an awareness of how it is affecting you personally. Once you reach this understanding, you will be ready to take steps to manage the stress caused by culture shock.

Culture shock is an emotional cycle with four distinct periods: enchantment, disenchantment, retreat, and adjustment. Although most people experience all four periods, each person's cycle is different; even different members of the same family will go through the ups and downs at different times.

Enchantment

Your arrival in your new home is an exciting time. Your senses are operating at top speed as you try to assimilate all of the new sights, sounds, and smells. You want to see and do everything. There are many new things to learn and discoveries to make. The differences that you notice between your home country and your new country are charming.

Disenchantment

After several weeks, a period of disenchantment typically sets in. As you establish your routine in your new country, reality begins to intrude on your enchantment. You have to deal with the mailman, the plumber, and your neighbors. Even simple tasks become difficult. When you go shopping, you may not recognize the food and you may not be able to find what you want and what you're used to. People may seem rude, overly friendly, or just plain different. It is emotionally taxing to speak a new language, to use a new currency, and to perform all of the other minor details that you never gave a second thought to at home. With the new reality comes a sense of frustration and irritation, and often insecurity, since all of the cues you never had to think about before have changed.

Retreat

As you begin to feel more and more frustrated, tension and resentment will begin to build up. The retreat stage of the adjustment cycle is the most difficult. It becomes harder to leave your home. If you work, you may find yourself working late or coming straight home from the office. You turn down invitations and minimize contact with the culture and people in the new country. What was once "charming" or "interesting" about the country and customs has become "strange" and "stupid." In the constant comparison between your home country and the host country, home wins hands down. Homesickness is acute.

Adjustment

Finally, you will have to make the effort to adjust, to reestablish contact with the world and go on with your life. Your attitude will determine how you reconcile yourself to the things that are different in your new country. The people who make the most successful adjustments are those who realize that there are things to like and dislike in any culture; doubtless there are things that you didn't care for at home, too. If you are willing to accept the culture, enjoy the things that you love about the culture and find ways to accommodate the parts that you do not like, you will be happy. Once you have managed a successful adaptation, you will realize that you have gained a new set of skills and are able to operate effectively within a new culture.

And Beyond

If you take another look at the Cultural Adjustment Curve, you will notice a second dip. Many people experience a second low period, or even a series of ups and downs. Just when you think you've finally got things figured out, you stumble again. A subsequent period of disillusionment might be more or less severe than the first; either reaction is normal.

KEYS TO A SUCCESSFUL ADJUSTMENT

The keys to a successful adjustment are self-awareness and acceptance. In order to be able to recognize cultural differences and effectively deal with them, you must first be aware of your own cultural values and attitudes.

Acceptance, the second key, means understanding that the culture, customs, and rules in your new country, however far from those of your home country, are valid. Once you are able to accept them as different rather than better or worse than your own, you will be more comfortable and able to adapt to new ways of doing things.

Understand that the ups and downs of cultural adjustment are normal; everyone who has moved before you has experienced the same process, complete with similar symptoms. If you reach out to those people, they can help you through the process. They will tell you that they survived and so will you.

Even after you have adjusted, you will have good days, when you feel at ease in your new culture, and bad days, when you question your sanity in deciding to move there. Once you have completely adjusted, the good days will eclipse the bad.

Coping Techniques

The psychological disorientation of an international move causes a tremendous amount of stress. In order to manage your cultural adaptation successfully, you must find an outlet for this stress. Think for a moment about how you relieve stress in your life right now. Stress outlets can be physical, such as jogging or biking, or mental, such as meditation or reading. List your stress relievers on a piece of paper. Once you've made your list, think about how you can continue those activities in your new home. Some of them—meditation, for instance—are easily transported. Some, however, may require modification or planning. For example, if you're used to riding your bike through the country lanes near your home but you will be moving to a crowded urban center, you may have to modify your activity. Can you use a stationary bike instead? Are there nearby parks or other areas where you can safely bike?

If you are not sure about the availability of a specific activity, make it a priority to find out. There are many resources, including other expats, people from your new country who may live in your area, consulates, books, and more.

FAMILIES

Families who have relocated to another country move with their own built-in support network to help each member through the process of adaptation. However, relocation also often means that family roles shift. A spouse who was a breadwinner before moving abroad might become a dependent; normally independent children may find themselves dependent on their parents, at least initially.

An international assignment often includes regional responsibilities that require frequent travel or extended business trips. If one partner is required to travel often, the other is left taking on more of the shared responsibilities in order to fill the gap left by the numerous absences. At times one feels like a single parent, even if it's not the case! Of course, the partner who is frequently away can find himself or herself feeling left out of the family upon returning.

All of these changes can be successfully managed if you have open lines of communication. Parents will benefit from talking with each other about the changes that are necessary to accommodate the new situation and by discussing ways that they can support each other to maintain consistency. The whole family will function better if everyone feels comfortable expressing fears and concerns and receives encouragement and support from other family members.

THE NONWORKING PARTNER

Unlike children and the working partner, a nonworking partner faces a new life that is without the inherent structure of school or work. So once the initial settling-in is done, your partner goes to work every day, the children traipse off to school, and you are left with nothing to do. If you were used to working, this is especially difficult. Even if you were not employed prior to the move, you still have left behind all of the familiar routines that filled your day.

According to article after article, many assignment failures are attributed to a nonworking partner who is unhappy in the new culture. This puts a lot of pressure on you; but with some effort and planning, you can put that particular worry aside.

In the absence of outside activities, the world of a nonworking partner is limited to household chores and the lives of children and the spouse. In the initial months, these same children and spouses have spent the majority of the day coping with their own stresses in the new culture and are rarely in the mood for scintillating conversation when they return to the sanctuary of home.

The more activities that you are involved in, the more fulfilled your own life will be. These activities can include your family, such as volunteering at your child's school, or they can be a pursuit of your own interests. The possibilities are practically endless. Other than volunteering, you can use the spare time to take classes, develop new skills, or pursue a hobby. If you give your imagination free rein, there are plenty of things that you can do. See the dual career sections throughout the book for other ideas on making the most of your time abroad.

CHILDREN

Children go through their own adjustment process, just as adults do. Younger children often feel frightened in a new location where everything is different from what they are used to: the people may look different, buildings may look different, and things certainly sound and smell different. Sometimes children (and adults, too) become an object of curiosity if they are living in a country where they look greatly different from the locals (for example, a blond child in Japan). They are often uncomfortable being stared at, touched, and patted by curious strangers. Younger children will have difficulty understanding what the move means and may tend to relate the move to vacations that they have experienced. They may be waiting for the trip to be over and for the family to return to their familiar surroundings at home. When the return home does not happen, they can get very upset. This may not happen for several weeks, or even months, so that a child who seems to have adjusted just fine may have problems down the road. Symptoms of their distress may be quite physical, such as stomachaches, or emotional, such as withdrawal and depression.

Older children, who do understand the implication of an international move and who realize that this move is not permanent, may be reluctant to get too deeply involved with friends, trying to protect themselves from the pain of making friends only to leave again after a year or two.

Throughout the process of adjustment, children will experience periods of anger. This is understandable since, in their minds, they may have been dragged across the world against their wishes. It is important to allow children, whatever their age, to express their anger and to provide them with appropriate outlets for it.

Keep in mind, too, that younger children may not be able to put their feelings into words. You can help them express their feelings by taking along children's books about moving that will help them find the words to tell you what is wrong.

Naturally, all children will react differently to an international move. The best way to cope is with patience and understanding.

Global Nomads and Third-Culture Kids

Global nomads, also called third-culture kids, are people who have lived overseas before adulthood, usually because of a parent's job. The global nomad is abroad without choice; the parents have chosen an international lifestyle, usually with the expectation that they will eventually return to the passport country. When children live abroad for a long period of time—or even for fairly short periods of time— they become culturally different from the parents. Their whole avenue of cultural exploration is very different from that of one born and reared in one place (as the parents often are).

Living internationally is a unique opportunity for children. It is a heritage that will shape the rest of their lives. While overseas, children develop a whole host of global skills, including multilingual skills, the ability to view situations from two different sides, and mediating and cross-cultural skills—simply by living. It is a heritage that can be applied very usefully in today's global arena.

One of the biggest challenges of moving abroad is maintaining the cultural identity of children. Children are absorbing the new culture through school, caregivers, and what they observe in the world around them. "Home" becomes a place to go on vacation once or twice a year. Parents can keep children connected to their own culture in a variety of ways, such as observing the holidays and traditions of their home culture. It is also helpful to keep in contact with what's going on at home, both with friends and family members and through magazines and newspapers.

PARENTING ABROAD

Raising a child abroad is a special challenge. Depending on where you are living, the values may be different from those you want to instill in your children. Children learn not only from their parents, but from school, peers, other caregivers, and society in general. Imagine that you have told your teenagers that they must be a certain age before they can drink, but they are suddenly confronted with vending machines in Japan which sell whiskey with no restrictions. This doesn't mean that Japan has a rampant problem with teenage alcoholism; it simply indicates that Japanese children are governed by different societal and parental restraints from your child's. These kinds of problems are best dealt with by establishing very clear family rules. Have family meetings to establish and reinforce the rules.

A lack of organized activities for teenagers is often a problem. You and your child may have to actively search for the activities he or she likes to do. If you can't find appropriate activities, think about organizing a baseball team, a drama group, or other activities yourself. Encourage your children to bring their friends over, and try to meet their friends' parents, just as you would at home.

In some countries, the expatriate life itself can pose hazards in the form of making children accustomed to a higher standard of living than most people. Some people find themselves in a position to obtain household help. If you have never had this experience, it will take some time to be comfortable having someone work for you. You may have to train the people you hire, and you should definitely be clear on your expectations; do not assume, for example, that your idea of disciplining your children is shared by the person you hire to babysit your child.

If you are lucky enough to have household help, you may find that your children come to expect that someone will pick up after them and believe that they are not personally responsible for any chores. You may want to continue to assign some household tasks to your children to reinforce your own values to them.

DUAL-CAREER COUPLES

Dual-career couples with children face the same issues as other families, but with an additional concern: child care. You are leaving behind your own child-care network and will have to rebuild it from scratch. This can be complicated in countries where the extended family plays a major role in child care and public or private care is rare. Even if your children are in school, there may not be structured activities for them to participate in during the time between school and the end of the work day. There are options if you search for them. Think about the following ideas:

- hire an au pair, nanny, or other live-in help
- look for formal or informal networks within the expat community; often there is a system of sharing child care
- if your job has the flexibility, work from home or part time
- approach a neighbor or another family about looking after your child during the day
- find an older person who would be interested in caring for your child (this has the added benefit of providing your child with a "grandparent")

If you are not able to find viable child-care options, you may be able to create something that will meet your needs. And there are sure to be other families who would welcome the alternative. Don't rule out starting a day-care center for younger children or organizing after-school activities for older children.

The most important thing, of course, is that you feel comfortable with your child-care arrangements and that you trust the person who will be caring for your children.

THE SINGLE LIFE

Living abroad as a single person has both ups and downs. Moving to a place where you have no network of friends is difficult; coping with a new country and culture where you may not know how to go about meeting people to create your new social network is even tougher. In many countries, a person's work and home lives are kept quite separate. Social bonds have been formed throughout the years in school and elsewhere; business relationships do not necessarily translate into social relationships. And, in many cases, the family and extended family play a significant role in a person's life, and a great deal of time is spent in family activities. All of this can make it seem impossible for a newly arrived person to meet people and form friendships.

On the other hand, expatriates are often not subject to the same "rules" as everyone else. Most expatriates find people in their host country to be very sympathetic to their situation, interested in learning more about them, and open to the possibilities of a relationship that extends beyond office hours. With luck, you will find yourself the recipient of invitations from your colleagues.

In the final analysis, though, it is up to you to build your new life. There are many avenues open to you. The best way to meet people, in fact, is to simply do something that you like to do. If you like to hike, go hiking; if you like to work out, join a gym. By doing something that interests you, you are putting yourself into situations where you can meet people with the same interests.

Another possibility to explore is the expatriate community. Where there are significant numbers of expatriates, there are usually networks in place, for both business and social purposes. Often there is a newcomers' club that provides activities and events for socializing. In these organizations, too, you will find people who have gone through the relocation and adaptation process and who have first-hand knowledge of what you are experiencing. These can be invaluable contacts throughout your own process of adaptation, giving you the support and encouragement you need, or even a shoulder to cry on when necessary.

Singles often have an especially rewarding experience abroad. Because they are not accompanied by a family, they generally have much more contact with the language and culture of the host country. An expat with a family goes home at the end of the day, speaks his or her native tongue at home, and is shielded from the language and culture to some extent. A single person does not have that shield, and spends more time speaking the new language and immersed in the culture through his or her social life. That person often has the added benefit of learning the language more quickly and thoroughly and of adapting to the new culture quickly.

THE GENDER FACTOR

The myth that women are not able to be successful in some cultures has largely been debunked. Instead, many experts say that, in fact, women are often better equipped to be successful than men. Most women find that they are viewed first and foremost as foreigners and are therefore not subject to all of the rules that apply to the local women. So even in cultures where women are not traditionally found in business, the same barriers may not apply to foreign women. In fact, many women have found that they can use the curiosity of local businessmen to their advantage and get their foot in the door more easily than their male counterparts.

One issue that women do face, on a very personal level, is whether or not they can accept the local culture—specifically the role and treatment of women. This does not mean that you have to behave exactly like the local women (although there may be a certain amount of conformity required of you), but you do have to be able to live with what is happening around you. This is a very personal decision; if you are uncomfortable with a culture's general attitude toward women, then perhaps it is better to wait for another assignment in a country where you feel more comfortable. Take care, though, that you understand the values that underlie the explicit behavior; it is easy to confuse the desire to protect with the desire to restrict.

THE RACE FACTOR

Most people of color find that they are seen first as being American, Canadian, British, etc. In countries where there is a history of discrimination against a certain minority group, usually an immigrant group, those rules simply do not apply to expatriates. There is no general formula for the experience that people of color have internationally. As in the case of one African-American, some expatriates feel that they actually have an advantage because they are used to being in the minority, which can make the adjustment to the new culture easier than for someone who is used to being part of the majority. As with the gender issue, it is not a question of the situation being good or bad; the issue is how you personally handle being in the limelight. In another case, a woman of Puerto Rican descent who grew up in New York considered herself to be an American and not a minority, with little thought of her cultural roots. When she was given an assignment in Latin America, she began to explore the Latino culture and to value that part of her heritage.

There are cases, however, where Americans of a particular minority group do encounter difficulty abroad. This occurs most often when a person relocates to his or her ancestral home. For example, a Japanese-American might be selected for an international assignment in Japan. Usually the selection is made because of the "Japanese" part of the equation, with little thought to the "American" part. In other words, the selection is made because someone looks the part. This strategy can backfire, though. Even if that person speaks Japanese, he has absorbed American culture and holds many American values since that is where he spent his formative years. The difficulty arises because he *looks* Japanese but does not *act* Japanese. The result can be suspicion, distrust, or ostracism on the part of the Japanese. Similar situations confront many Asian-Americans whose families immigrated generations ago, including "overseas Chinese," and Vietnamese-Americans. These issues can be minimized or avoided if you have an awareness of who you are and an understanding of the culture that you will be living in, especially the ways in which it is different from your own blended culture.

SEXUAL ORIENTATION

If you are lesbian or gay, you will probably want to do some research on the acceptance of homosexuals in the country you will be living in before you embark on your international assignment. While some countries have laws preventing discrimination against anyone because of sexual orientation, the acceptance of homosexuals by the society in general ranges from tolerance to homophobia much as it does in the United States. Make sure you are also aware of any laws prohibiting homosexual acts, and the possible consequences of practicing your sexuality. These concerns will affect bisexuals and transgendered people as well.

In Germany, homosexuality is openly discussed and widely accepted. However, this does not mean that you will not experience discrimination if you are open with your sexuality, especially in small towns.

Moving abroad with a same-sex partner presents certain challenges not faced by married partners, as it is virtually impossible for an accompanying partner to get a work visa without being legally married. However, all German states have a domestic partnership law, which grants same-sex partners the same rights as a married couple.

As an accompanying partner, you must focus on the alternatives that are available to you in the new country. Issues of giving up or postponing a career must be dealt with, and work alternatives must be investigated. Be proactive in exploring your options. Try to talk to people who have experience living in the country, both natives of the country and expatriates who have lived there. The more people you can talk to, the more complete a picture you will have of the implications of being lesbian, gay, bisexual or transgendered in your new culture.

A WORD ABOUT "EXPATRIATE CLUBS"

Many expats are wary of expatriate clubs, seeing them as a group of spouses who get together to play tennis and bridge. Even if there are people in the organization who do play bridge, the clubs are much more than that. Expat organizations are an excellent source of information on everyday issues such as finding a doctor, and offer networking, which accompanying partners who are seeking jobs or alternatives can tap into, a chance to learn about the culture through structured activities and events, and socializing. Each individual can decide how much he or she wants to be involved in the expatriate community. Indeed, there are plenty of expats who immerse themselves in it and have very little contact with local-country nationals. There are also people who avoid it altogether. You are free to choose either, or any point in the spectrum between. Just keep in mind that the expatriate network can be invaluable; it can also provide that touch of home when you need it.

STAYING IN TOUCH

Even if you are excited about the prospect of living abroad, don't forget to make plans to stay in touch. You will want to hear from your family and friends at home, and keep them up to date on your own adventures. It's very easy to get swept up in your new life, and difficult to find the time to write or call with all of the new challenges of living abroad. However, the people who form your network of support will continue to be important as you adjust to your life abroad, especially during difficult times.

Establishing and maintaining a systematic way of communicating with home is also critical when it comes time to return after your sojourn abroad—something that is difficult to think about when you haven't even left yet!

ROUND-TRIP TICKET: THE RETURN HOME

Contrary to what you might think, the return home, or repatriation, after an international assignment is often a more difficult transition than moving abroad.

Professional Repatriation

One of the hazards of living and working internationally is that when you return you can find yourself out of touch with your home office and with changes in your field or profession. Without proper preparation, you may find yourself without an office, without direction, and, indeed, without a job. Many former expats have returned to the home country after a successful assignment only to have to wait for a suitable position to open up. In addition, many returned expatriates find that their experience abroad, and newly acquired skills and knowledge, are not put to use by the organization. A marketing manager fresh from an assignment in Latin America may find herself in a domestic marketing position, with little or no involvement in any Latin American markets. Even if the goal of the assignment was your professional development with an eye toward "globalization" or developing the international market, it is difficult to put those lofty goals to work practically. It is up to you to ensure that you are receiving the support you need during the assignment and to plan your strategy for reintegration into the home or local office.

If you moved abroad with your partner but were unable to work abroad, you face some of the same challenges when you return. You may feel that technology has passed you by, or that the skills you used before you moved are rusty from disuse. The best way to counteract this is to think about coming home while you are abroad and make sure that you keep your skills up to date—and maybe even develop new skills or expertise!

Following these steps can ease your professional reentry:

- Set a strategy before you go. Getting the support of upper management is crucial. Make sure you have a clear understanding of the objective of sending you abroad, what your goals are during the assignment, and exactly how you will fit back into the organization when you return.

- Stay in touch while you are abroad. In the case of international assignees, "out of sight, out of mind" holds true more often than not. Remind the home office of all of the points outlined above. Keep them informed about your activities and your accomplishments. And keep yourself informed about what is going on at the home office: promotions and staff changes, important policy changes, etc. E-mail and faxes are readily available in most companies; take advantage of technology to maintain contact.

- Find a mentor. In fact, find two or three. Mentors will help keep you in the minds of the decision-and policy-makers and keep you informed about what's going on at home. Mentoring relationships do not have to be formalized. And with several mentors you won't find yourself returning from your assignment only to find that your champion in the company no longer works there!

- Visit the home office whenever you can. While you are on a home leave or business trip back, take the opportunity to reconnect with colleagues. Make use of the time to familiarize yourself with recent changes. Even if you take all of the recommended steps to stay in touch, understand that things will be different when you return. The fact is, the company and your colleagues have grown in the time you have been away, just as you have. It will take time and patience to reintegrate yourself into the new environment.

Personal Repatriation

Personal repatriation can also be painful. During your sojourn, you will have gained new insights and new perspectives. You will realize that there is really no right or wrong way to do things, only different ways. In addition, most people remember "home" with fondness while they are away, forgetting about the things that aren't so great. And, of course, you will come home to find that your home country has its share of blemishes, just like everywhere else. This means that you will go through another cycle of adjustment as you refamiliarize yourself with your home culture and come to terms with the bad as well as the good in it.

If you are gone for several years, you will experience some disorientation when you return. Things will have changed, and you will have had a long period of time when you have not shared experiences with your family and friends. You may find that some people aren't interested in hearing about your experiences abroad, or who roll their eyes when you say "When I was in...." You may even encounter people who feel that you are putting on airs or that you feel superior because of your experience. You will have to come to terms with the fact that the people you knew before you left have changed, as you have, but in different ways.

There are ways to ease your personal readjustment.

- Stay in touch while you are gone. This can be difficult as you immerse yourself in your new life. Just as you fade from prominence at home, home fades for you. You will have to make a conscious effort to maintain regular contact, and to make sure your kids do. The benefit of doing this is that when you return there is less of a void in your experiences; you have kept people informed of important events in your lives, and vice versa.

- Visit home whenever possible. This is especially important if you have children. As well as helping you keep in contact with friends and family, it helps children maintain their sense of "home" and their cultural identity.

- Realize that your return home will have its ups and downs, just as your adjustment to living abroad did.

Children's Repatriation

The most difficult part of readjustment for children is that they have a gap in their lives where they have missed all of the pieces of popular culture that their friends have experienced, such as music, movies, TV, toys, and the way kids dress. They have to learn the current slang. Along with this, they are different from their peers. They have developed in ways that kids at home have not, and they have a different frame of reference. More than adults, children who return home after living abroad will find that their peers see them as thinking that they are superior and resent references to "When I was in...."

Tips for Staying in Touch

Most of us are accustomed to picking up the telephone and calling someone whenever we want. If you are living in another country, though, you may find that this isn't as easy any more because of time differences, poor phone service, or the prohibitive cost of international calls. Here are some suggestions for alternative ways of staying in touch, either with your home country when you're abroad, or with your host country after you've left.

- **The old stand-by: write letters.** Since the advent of the telephone, most of us are no longer letter writers. When phoning is too expensive, this is one of the cheapest alternatives. However, it's also the slowest!

- **Fax letters.** Write your letter, then fax it. This will give you the satisfaction of instantaneous communication, without the prohibitive cost of an extended telephone call. Family and friends without a fax machine can probably arrange to receive faxes at a nearby copy shop or similar service center.

- **E-mail.** Probably the least expensive alternative. Almost every business in Germany has Internet access. Keep in mind that a private connection is about 3 times as expensive as it is in America.

- **Chatting online.** If you and your family/friends all have

Internet access, and you are able to access the Internet from your new country, try scheduling a time to find a quiet on-line corner to chat. Some of the larger services such as MSN and AOL offer service in Germany. Just remember that you may have to pay for local connect time rates—check with your service provider.

- **Use the company's phone.** With the company's permission, of course! As part of the expatriate package, some companies will allow you and your family members limited use of office phones to make international calls.

- **Videotapes or cassettes.** Although they will take a while to get there, videotapes and cassettes are more personal than writing letters. It's especially nice if you have children. You can exchange tapes with family members, and your children can exchange them with friends and even their classes at school. Be sure you will have access to the right equipment, since Germany uses PAL instead of NTSC. A further word of caution: be careful not to run afoul of the local laws. For example, in some countries, a videotape that includes your sister frolicking on the beach in a bikini may be considered pornography locally, even if you don't think it is. Make sure you know all of the applicable laws.

- **Write a newsletter.** This is especially helpful if you've got a long list of people you want to keep in contact with. Document what is going on in your life: write about the funny things that happen, current events in your new community, or anything else that appeals. Or start a round-robin letter, where everyone who receives the letter adds to it and passes it on to the next person.

- **Schedule regular phone calls.** It's bad enough to reach an answering machine when you want to talk to someone. It's worse when you are paying international rates to talk to a machine! If you talk to someone often, try to arrange for a regular time to call—every Sunday night at 10:00, the last Saturday of each month, or whatever fits both of your schedules.

LEARNING ABOUT YOUR NEW HOME

You're on your way to a new adventure. Now is the time to gather all of the information you need to make your international sojourn successful. Learning the language (if it's different from yours) and learning about the culture of your new home should be prioritized.

Learning the language of the country you will be living in is an obvious necessity. If it happens to be a language you already speak, great; if not, get started as soon as possible. Make it your goal to learn at least basic phrases before you go, more if possible. This book comes complete with a special language section and an audio CD for just that. While some people have a facility for learning languages, others find it more difficult. And it is often more difficult for adults than for children. Yes, you will make mistakes, and even embarrass yourself. It will be frustrating to have to struggle to express yourself, and you will feel awkward speaking with a limited vocabulary as you start out, but the effort is well worth it. The fact that you are willing to make the effort to adjust yourself to a new language will open many doors for you, and you will find that most people respond with delight. Learning the language also gives you the opportunity to really experience life in the local community in ways that are not possible if you are isolated from interaction by not speaking the local language.

Just as important as learning the language of your new country is learning about its culture and peoples. What are the values that the people hold, what is their history, what are their beliefs, customs, and traditions? In the Background section of this book, we've provided you with enough of this kind of information to whet your appetite. Don't stop there, though! There are lots of ways to go about learning about the culture of your new country, including reading books and articles, talking to other expats or people from the country, and participating in a pre-departure (or post-arrival!) cultural orientation. Don't expect to learn everything there is to learn about the country in such a short time, or imagine that you will be prepared for every contingency; your goal is to learn enough to be comfortable in your new home. Once you arrive, you will discover on your own much more than you can ever learn from a book or from talking to other people.

Perhaps the first step in learning about your new culture is to learn about yourself and your own culture. Because culture is such a deeply-rooted part of who we are, few people take the time to ponder what it is that makes them tick. Spend some time reflecting on your own cultural heritage, and ask yourself the same questions you would ask of another culture: What are *your* values, what is *your* history, what are *your* beliefs, customs and traditions? The more you understand about yourself, the easier it will be for you to recognize cultural differences and reduce the likelihood of cultural misunderstandings.

Moving Abroad "DOS AND DON'TS"

DO...
...have realistic expectations
...find out as much as you can before you go
...learn the language—at least basic phrases
...be open-minded
...find several mentors and cultural guides

DON'T...
...lose touch with family and friends; make plans now
    for keeping in touch
...wait until it is time to return to plan for your repatriation
...wait for other people to come to you; take the initiative
    and reach out

FOUR

GETTING AROUND

Whether you're visiting Germany for a short time or living there for an extended period, you've got to be able to get from Point A to Point B. A lot of the information you'll need is straightforward and pretty much what you would expect. But there are some important differences between the United States and Germany to keep in mind. This chapter provides simple tips and practical information on driving, rules of the road, public transportation, and taxis.

DRIVING

Germany is famous for its Autobahn, perhaps the best road network in all of Europe and even beyond. This section will help you navigate the twisting streets of any medieval town or race from Hamburg to Munich on the Autobahn. Speaking of racing on the Autobahn, that's the first thing that comes to the minds of many Americans when they think about driving on Germany's highways: speed. But before we get to the rules of the road, let's cover the basics.

If you need to rent a car, you'll find that it's not difficult, but it will probably be expensive. Simply call the rental company to reserve a car. Credit cards are accepted. You will recognize the names of many major international car rental companies, such as Hertz and Avis. As in the United States, there are rental companies at every major airport and in all major cities.

Liability insurance is required for all cars. In addition, most financial institutions require collision and/or comprehensive insurance as well before they will finance the purchase of an automobile. For safety purposes, you must have a warning triangle and first-aid kit in your car, and all persons in the vehicle, front or back, must wear a seatbelt. Children under the age of 12 require special seats. It may be advisable to purchase a child's seat in Germany to ensure compliance with German regulations.

Every German city has a *Kraftfahrzeugsamt* (KFZ-Amt). This office deals with all vehicular concerns, from registering your auto to getting a new driver's license. You can contact your local KFZ-Amt with any questions you have about your vehicle or driver's license.

Parking tickets are issued by a department of the *Verkehrspolizei*, the Traffic Police. You will be ticketed if you park illegally, including in a bicycle lane or fire zone. Your car may be towed if it is illegally parked in such a way as to be a potential hazard.

American and Canadian citizens living in Germany for less than a year can use a driver's license from their home country or an international driver's license. Any non-German license, however, must be accompanied by a German translation. You can obtain a translation from the local office of the *Allgemeiner Deutscher Automobilclub* (ADAC), Germany's premier automobile club, similar to the AAA in the United States. You can obtain an international driver's license from the AAA in the United States for a small fee, even if you are not a member.

If you are living in Germany for more than one year, however, you will need to get a German *Führerschein* (driver's license) as soon as you arrive. Seventeen states in the United States currently have an agreement with Germany that allows drivers to simply swap their U.S. license for a German one. You can check with your local motor vehicle office or with the German consulate to see if your state has such a reciprocal agreement.

If you are not fortunate enough to live in one of these states, you will need to attend a *Fahrschule* (driving school) and take a first aid course. You must take both a written and practical driving test, as well as a vision test. The written test is available in English. Many driving schools offer an abbreviated course for experienced drivers. The cost for a full driving course is usually about 1,250 EUR; an abbreviated course will cost about 230 EUR.

Driver's licenses are issues by the local county government (*Landratsamt*). You will need the following documentation: an application, your passport, an *Aufenthaltserlaubnis* (residence permit), two passport-size photos, your current driver's license and its German translation, proof that you attended a *Fahrschule*, proof of completion of the required first-aid course, and proof of a vision test from an optometrist or the TÜV—*Technischer Überwachungsverein* (Technical Supervision Association). Keep in mind that you will have to give up your American license for several weeks during this process, a time in which you will not be able to drive.

You will need to register your vehicle at the *Autozulassungsstelle* (Motor Vehicle Registry). To do so, you will need proof of ownership and the *Kraftfahrzeugbrief* (Motor Vehical Document) (if the car was purchased in Germany). Most dealers will handle the vehicle registration.

Car inspections are also necessary, and quite strict. Newly purchased cars must be inspected after three years and every two years thereafter. Inspections are conducted by the TÜV.

Rules of the Road

Following are some of the basic rules of the road. Be sure to contact the proper authorities for a complete guide to the rules and regulations governing driving in Germany.

- Unless indicated, there is no speed limit on the autobahn. The recommended maximum safe driving speed, however, is 130 kph (80 mph). Accidents occurring at speeds greater than 130 kph often result in the cancellation of your insurance policy, regardless of fault.
- In and around cities and on other roads there are posted speed limits. Many places have cameras that take a picture of your license plate if you are speeding; your ticket will arrive in the mail.
- If you are unlucky enough to be stopped for speeding, you can pay in cash on the spot or you can elect to receive the ticket by mail. Simply fill out the enclosed *Überweisung* (bank transfer form) and mail it to your bank, where the money will be taken out of your account. Or, if you wish to pay in cash, take the *Überweisung* to the bank to pay.
- A point system is used to track violations. Penalties become

increasingly severe with the number of violations, especially if drugs or alcohol were involved or if an accident occurred.

- Unless otherwise indicated, the vehicle on the right has the right of way at intersections.

- The left lane is for passing only; drive in the far right lane unless you are passing another vehicle. This is especially important on the Autobahn, where people drive very fast. Because of the speed of traffic, be careful not to underestimate the speed of approaching cars in the left lane as you go to pass. Passing another vehicle on the right is a very serious violation.

- Because of the higher driving speed, multivehicle accidents on the Autobahn are not uncommon and are frequently deadly. Defensive driving is a must, especially on the autobahn.

- A car behind you blinking its headlights wants you to get out of its way. Most Germans have little patience for inconsiderate drivers, so this is not a request but a demand.

- It is illegal to turn right at a red light, even if there is no crossing traffic. In the eastern states and—very rarely—in some western states, some traffic lights display a green arrow which allows you to turn right during a red light.

- Watch out for bicycle traffic. Cyclists should be regarded as equal to other vehicles and operate under the same rules. Many cities have a bicycle lane running alongside the road; these are one-way lanes matching the flow of traffic.

- Pedestrians should be given the right of way whenever possible. However, many drivers do not stop at pedestrian crosswalks. When you stop for pedestrians, be sure that traffic behind you isn't too close to stop.

- If you are driving in a city that has streetcars, be aware that they make frequent stops in the middle of the street. You cannot pass the streetcar, and must wait until the passengers disembark and move off the road.

- Don't drink and drive! Good advice anywhere, but the blood-alcohol ratio in Germany is much lower than elsewhere (0.5 mg per 100 ml of blood), and some people are over the limit after only one beer.

- If you are stopped by the police, you will be asked for your driver's license and the documents for your vehicle (*Wagenpapiere*).

- In case of an automobile accident, you are legally obliged to warn other vehicles by turning on your hazard lights and placing a warning triangle (always carry one of these in the trunk of your car) in a visible location. You must also provide first aid if necessary. Germans get first-aid training as part of their mandatory driver's training. If you will be driving a lot in Germany, consider signing up for a first-aid class. Keep in mind that you can be sued for not providing first aid when needed or for causing injury by improperly administering first aid.

- If you are in an automobile accident, you will want to notify the police. Exchange the following information with anyone else involved: vehicle license number, driver's name and address, driver's insurance company. You may also get the names and addresses of any witnesses.

ON FOOT

- The first rule of being a pedestrian in Germany is to obey the traffic signals. The police frequently ticket for jaywalking. At the very least, you can expect that fellow pedestrians will point out to you the error of your ways.
- Although pedestrians should have the right of way, don't assume that a driver will stop at a pedestrian crossing zone; be sure any oncoming cars will halt before you start across.

PUBLIC TRANSPORTATION

Getting around in Germany is quick and easy. You can easily find a reliable public transport stop within a few kilometers of almost anywhere. There are many ways you can greatly reduce your travel expenses. Following are some options:

- *BahnCard*—If you are living in Germany, you are entitled to travel at a 25% discount for the year with the purchase of this card. The *BahnCard* costs 60 EUR for 2nd class and 150 EUR for 1st class.
- *Mitfahrer-Rabatt*—Up to 4 people can travel together for half price.
- *Plan&Spar*—Book ahead and save: booking one day ahead saves 10%, three days ahead saves 25%, and seven days ahead with a Saturday night stay saves 40%.
- *Family travel discounts*—Children under 14 travel for free. Also, if one parent owns a *BahnCard,* their partner and children under 17 can get a *BahnCard* for only 5 EUR.
- *German Rail Pass**—Non-Europeans can get unlimited travel within Germany for 4 to 10 consecutive days at a set price (number of days and class of travel will alter the price).
- *Eurail Pass**—The Eurail Pass is good for unlimited travel throughout 17 European countries during a specified block of time.

For the most current information on German rail prices, visit **www.bahn.de.**

* Note: These tickets must be purchased outside of Germany. Check with your local travel agent for pricing, details, and restrictions.

Germany has excellent intercity and local train systems. The national train system is the Deutsche Bundesbahn or DB. Trains are frequent: at least one per hour (usually more) from early morning until late evening. Express trains between large cities (ICE trains) are quite frequent. These modern trains travel at speeds up to 150 mph; they are air-conditioned and have phones, faxes, and sometimes music or films available. There is usually a surcharge for express trains. Intercity (IC) trains, while not as fast as ICE trains, serve some 40 cities and towns in Germany. Regular DB trains provide local links to smaller towns and are slower than ICE or IC trains.

Seat reservations are available at no extra charge on ICE and IC lines, and can make traveling a long distance easier. Before sitting down, make sure your targeted seat isn't reserved (*reserviert*); if it is, it will have a small card above the seat next to the seat number or in the window of the compartment. You may sit in a reserved seat only if the passenger who reserved it will not be boarding until after you disembark. For example, if you are traveling from Stuttgart to Heidelberg on the Stuttgart–Frankfurt line, and a seat is reserved from Heidelberg to Frankfurt, you may take the seat.

You can buy your train ticket at the train station or at travel agents (with no fees or surcharges) authorized by the DB. Authorized agents usually display a sign in the window. In an emergency, you can buy the ticket from the conductor, but there will be a surcharge.

Most trains have both enclosed compartments (six seats per compartment) and open cars. If you make a reservation, you can request smoking or non-smoking. Traveler beware, though: don't reserve a seat in a smoking car unless you are well and truly prepared to sit in a smoke-filled environment.

Many large cities have an electric streetcar system (*Straßenbahn* or *S-Bahn*) or subway (*Untergrundbahn* or *U-Bahn*). Local transportation fares vary according to distance. Buy your ticket at a machine before boarding, and punch it in the machine at the entrance of the *U-Bahn* or on the bus. Buying your ticket from a machine can be intimidating if you don't read German, as the directions appear only in German, so take some time to figure out the local transportation system. Tickets are usually valid on all transportation systems and good for a transfer.

Germany has two types of bus service: one operated by the Deutsche Bundesbahn and one operated by the city itself. Bus schedules are generally coordinated with train and streetcar schedules. On some local buses you can pay the driver when you get on; many accept correct change only. Intercity bus tickets can be purchased at a travel agency.

Tips for a Smooth Ride

- Most local transportation stops running overnight. Be sure you check to see when the last train leaves or you will have to return by taxi.
- Payment is largely on the honor system; a random ticket check that catches you without a properly validated ticket will net you a hefty fine.
- When using public transportation and in other public places, Germans are generally reserved, preferring quiet decorum to loud or boisterous conversation.
- When on the subway, train, or bus, it is good manners for men to give up their seat for women and for people to yield their seats to the elderly, the disabled, or pregnant women.

TAXIS

You can recognize a taxi by the light on top, which is illuminated when the taxi is free. German taxis are quite impressive, especially for those who have only experienced the taxis in large metropolitan areas in the United States. They are mostly Mercedes, or other expensive models, and they are generally very clean and well-kept.

Taxis are common in both big cities and villages. In the former they may be hailed or met at a taxi stand in central areas. If no taxi stand is available, or if you would like to make an appointment, you can call the taxi company to make arrangements.

The taxi driver may or may not speak English. If you don't speak German, you can write down your destination and give it to the driver. Your fare will be clearly displayed on the meter. Tipping is optional, although most people round up the fare or add an extra mark or so, depending on the fare. Note, though, that there is usually a small extra charge for luggage and dogs.

FIVE

LIVING AND STAYING IN GERMANY

Whether you're moving to Germany for several years or just staying for a few months, either on business or for personal reasons, this section will show you the nuts and bolts of everyday life. Here you'll learn how to avoid the pitfalls of housing, using telephones, dining, and socializing. This section contains a lot of useful information even if you're spending just a day or two in Germany, so read on. The bottom line is that you will be interacting with Germans on some level, no matter how long your stay. Here's how to make that interaction enjoyable for everyone.

By the Way ...

WELL PRESERVED

A friend of mine was invited to dinner by a German family. After a lovely meal, she tried to express her appreciation. What she wanted to say was that the meal was deli-
cious and that she loved the food in Germany, because it
was fresh and didn't have any preservatives. Since she
didn't know how to say "preservatives" in German, she
just Germanized the English word, coming up with
Präservative. Unfortunately for her, that particular word is
a false cognate—that is, a word that sounds like an
English word but has a different meaning in fact. Much to
her chagrin, she learned after everyone finally stopped
laughing that she had praised German food for having no
condoms in it.

German and English have many words that sound
alike, and indeed share a meaning in many cases, such
as garden/*Garten* and house/*Haus*. Don't let this lull you
into a sense of complacency, though. There are plenty of
false cognates. For example, if you want to give someone
ein Gift, you're actually trying to poison him or her. *Das
Gift* is poison, and gift is *das Geschenk*. And if you're feeling blue, you'd better not say *Ich bin blau*, because that
means that you're drunk.

HOUSING

If you're not planning on renting or buying a home, you may want
to skip ahead to the section Bringing Your Belongings.

Finding a Living Space

It can be quite a challenge to locate an apartment or home in Germany, so give yourself plenty of time. As elsewhere, there are three ways to go about finding a place to live: newspaper ads, a real-estate agent, and word of mouth. Don't discount word of mouth; it's often more reliable than newspaper ad leads and it's always cheaper than an agent!

You'll need to have some basic information for your search. Because most foreigners living in Germany for a limited time find themselves renting, this section refers to apartment living. However, most of the information applies if you are in the market to buy as well. Where appropriate we have included the abbreviations that you might see in an advertisement.

Most local newspapers carry real-estate ads on Wednesdays and Saturdays. Be prepared, however, to find that it's not easy to get in touch with the person who placed the ad, since many people do not have answering machines, or that the apartment has been taken by the time you do manage to get through.

If you want to go the real-estate-agent (*Immobilienmakler* or *Makler*) route, which is probably the quickest, be prepared to shell out the equivalent of up to three months' rent for his or her services. This way, however, you have a guarantee that everything is compliant with the law.

The vast majority of apartments come unfurnished. Furnished (*möbl.=möbliert*) apartments are few and far between, and are very expensive. Apartments are listed by the number of rooms, excluding the kitchen, halls, and bathrooms/toilets, or in square meters (*qm=m²=quadratmeter*).

Most unfurnished apartments in Germany are really that: unfurnished. Almost every apartment has a kitchen sink, the basic bathroom equipment, light fixtures, and often a stove. Sometimes built-in closets are included, but a refrigerator is uncommon. If the landlord requests a deposit, the apartment has to be in mint condition.

There is still a difference in the quality of many apartments in the states of former East Germany, especially in larger cities. However, the rent is considerably lower, and they are usually fully renovated when they become vacant.

The vast majority of apartments have central heating (*Heizung*), a bathroom with bathtub (*Bad*) and/or shower (*Dusche*), and toilet (*WC*).

If you don't want to get an apartment through an agent, be aware that many of the offers in papers might be subleases or have some other downside. Most serious landlords go through an agency. A former tenant might ask for a compensation (*Abstand*) for furniture left behind, which is not quite legal, but not uncommon.

In addition to the real-estate agent's fee, you will face a security deposit (*Ka, Kt* or *Kaut=Kaution*), usually another two to three months' rent. You can get the *Kaution* back when you leave the apartment, but don't count on it. You have to leave the apartment in very good condition, and you may be responsible for some renovations or repairs.

On top of your monthly rent, you might be responsible for paying the *Nebenkosten* (utilities), which may or may not be included in your rent payment but covers things like heating. Be sure to find out exactly what is included in your rent. While your rent is stable for the duration of the contract, the *Nebenkosten* can be raised.

Other utilities and services (electricity, gas, telephone, etc.) are paid for separately by the tenant. Go to the local *Stadtwerke* (city power plant) office to get your gas and electricity turned on, and Deutsche Telekom for phone service. If you get the apartment through an agency, this should all be taken care of for you. Be forewarned that it can take up to two weeks to install a phone line, so if you are able to take over the previous tenant's line, it is advisable to do so. (Note: Deutsche Telekom has a monopoly on the phone lines. As a result, cellular phones have become quite popular, and can often be cheaper than a Telekom line.)

Make sure you officially cancel all utilities and services when you leave your apartment or house. If you don't, you may find yourself receiving bills for a long, long time after you leave.

As a last note, rental contracts are often intricate and complicated; it is wise to seek help from a knowledgeable friend or the *Makler*, or even a lawyer (*Rechtsanwalt* or *Notar*). German laws strongly protect the rights of a tenant; once a contract is signed, there is little the owner can do to remove an occupant. You should make an effort to become aware of the provisions and clauses in your housing contract. Also note that if you have a pet, you'll need to get written permission from your landlord to keep it in your apartment or house.

PERMISSION GRANTED?

So you've found a place to live. Think you're all set? Think again!

If you wish to live in Germany for more than three months, you must obtain a residence permit (*Aufenthaltserlaubnis*) and a confirmation of registration (*Anmeldebestätigung*) from the local authorities at the Foreign Nationals Office (*Ausländeramt*). This may turn into a rather long affair, since you have to first obtain the forms and make sure you have all of the required proofs (listed below), then register in person (although one person can register the whole family).

The documents one needs for an *Aufenthaltserlaubnis* vary from town to town, but in general you will need the following. Contact the local office for information specific to your location.

- A certificate of good conduct, stating that you have not been convicted of a crime (obtainable from the U.S. embassy or consulate)
- Proof of health insurance
- Proof that you have a place to live
- Proof that you have a job or can otherwise support yourself financially
- A health certificate (*Gesundheitszeugnis*) from a German doctor or public health facility (you may have to provide the form to your doctor)

If you will be working in Germany, you must specifically state that fact on the application for the *Aufenthaltserlaubnis*; otherwise your passport might automatically get stamped that you are not eligible to work, and the *Arbeitsamt* (labor office) will not be able to issue you a work permit.

The *Anmeldebestätigung* is proof that you are a resident of your community, and you will need it for many things, including registering your children for school or getting a library card. When you move, whether across the street or across the country, you will need to unregister (*abmelden*) at your old location and reregister at the new location. Don't take the need for an *Anmeldebestätigung* personally—Germans as well as foreigners are obliged to keep the authorities informed of their place of residence.

By the Way ...

LAST NIGHT I SLEPT LIKE A ... MARMOT?

Yes, you heard right. If you tell your German friends that you have *wie ein Hund geschlafen* (slept like a dog), they won't know what you're talking about. Tell them that you slept like a marmot (*ein Murmeltier*) instead. The marmot (the German version of a groundhog), is one of the few animals in Germany that goes into hibernation. Similarly, if your friend says that you're taking him *auf den Arm* (on the arm), don't take him literally and think you're leading him somewhere. He means that you're pulling his leg. Of course if you told him that in German, he'd be a bit perplexed. And although we could go on forever with these mixed-up idiomatic expressions, let's end with just one more. When you hear someone described this way: *Er/Sie hat nicht alle Tassen im Schrank* (he/she doesn't have all his/her cups in the cupboard), don't wonder who broke the fine china. This means the same thing as saying that someone isn't playing with a full deck, doesn't have both oars in the water, has all the lights on but nobody's home...you get the picture.

BRINGING YOUR BELONGINGS

Of course you will want to bring the things that will make your new house or apartment feel like home. It is important, though, to think things through before you start packing. Consider the fact that your appliances and electronic equipment will need to be adapted to both the German electrical voltage and the plug configuration, and even then they may not work at peak performance because of the differ-

ence in hertz values. Many people moving to Germany find it preferable to leave most of their appliances at home (or sell them) and apply the money they would have spent moving them to purchasing new equipment once they arrive.

A second option is to contact a company that specializes in furnishing appliances that meet international specifications. This will allow you to purchase your appliances before leaving and arrange for their delivery to your new home, saving you the hassle of shopping in an unfamiliar environment, especially when you will probably have a million other things to do to get settled.

Remember that German measurements are based on metrics. (See Appendix C for metric conversions.) This will impact on your life in more ways than you can imagine. For example, if you are taking your family's beds with you, German fitted linens won't fit, so you will need to take your linen with you or be prepared to use flat sheets only. The same applies, of course, if you are bringing items purchased in Germany back with you.

BRINGING YOUR VEHICLE

Although it is certainly possible to bring over your own vehicle, you should do some research on the subject first. German emissions laws are very stringent, and most foreign cars will need to have rather extensive modifications (to the catalytic converter, for example) to ensure compliance. The cost of conversion and transport generally make purchasing a car in Germany the more attractive alternative.

If you do decide to bring your vehicle, you will need to register it in Germany, pay applicable taxes and registration fees, and, in some cases, have it inspected for compliance with safety and technical regulations. You can contact the *Bundesamt für Kraftfahrzeuge* (Federal Vehicle Office) in Flensburg for further information.

RULES, RULES, RULES

There are many rules you will have follow when you are living in Germany. Some of these are laws, while others are more along the lines of standards preventing behavior that is taboo or frowned upon. Don't think that the "frowned upon" activities are merely guidelines, however; your neighbors will complain, either to you, to your landlord, or even to the police, if you break the rules. You can check with the local authorities, your landlord, or your neighbors for rules specific to your building, neighborhood, or city, but here is a sampling of what to expect:

- Trash must go in special receptacles provided by the landlord. You might have to separate your trash (food waste, wrapping, etc.) Recyclables are further separated into glass (by color), plastic, paper, and metals.
- For disposal of large items you must contact the sanitation office. There are scheduled *Sperrmüll* days for special and large

items, or you might be able to make an appointment for a special pickup.

- Don't leave bicycles or other items in hallways or areas not specifically designated by the landlord.
- Germany has mandatory quiet hours: 1–3 PM daily; 10 PM–7 AM Monday to Saturday; all day Sunday.
- It is generally expected that people do not mow lawns, wash cars, or otherwise disturb the peace on Sundays.
- You cannot wash your car on the street.

NEIGHBORS OR FRIENDS

Borgen macht Sorgen.
Borrowing makes worries.

While Germans don't have any compunction about monitoring your public behavior, they also have a great respect for privacy. Neighbors generally keep to themselves, and the average German would never consider going to the neighbor's house to borrow a cup of sugar. While you certainly want to be cordial to your neighbors, don't assume that proximity will lead to friendship. Here are a few tips on keeping peace with your neighbors.

- Introduce yourself to your neighbors.
- Always be polite when you see your neighbors, but not intrusive or overfriendly.
- Observe quiet hours. This is not only a courtesy, it is the law!
- Keep the hallways clear of all items, such as bicycles, skates, etc.
- If you are planning on having a party, inform your neighbors, especially if you are living in an apartment. You may even want to invite them.

SHOPPING

Shopping in another country is always an interesting experience. In Germany, you will find most of the goods you are used to seeing at home, but there will also be many new things for you to try. Although some European products are becoming available in the United States, most American children (and adults) have never tried Nutella®, a chocolate and hazelnut spread commonly found on European breakfast tables. Many an American has quickly become addicted to the stuff.

Sometimes you will find that the items you are familiar with a) have a different name, b) aren't readily available in Germany, or c) are available, but not immediately recognizable in their local form. Diet Coke®, for example, is Coke Light® (written, oddly enough, in

English; it also tastes a little bit different). Peanut butter is hard to come by, and you won't find a vast array of sugary cereal available (children are the only people at the breakfast table with a bowl of cereal in most German homes). Celery, on the other hand, does exist, but Germans eat the leafy part of the plant rather than the stalk, and most asparagus is white, not green. In general, though, if you are flexible you will eventually find everything you need—you will even expand your tastes.

American brands can be found in larger supermarkets, but are often more expensive. If you or your family are attached to a particular item or brand, you might want to stock up and ship a quantity to your new home. Once you familiarize yourself with the aisles of your local supermarket, however, you will be able to find local products at a more reasonable price.

There are many different types of stores in Germany. Although supermarkets do exist, most people still visit their local butcher, baker, greengrocer, and other specialty shops individually. This is in part due to the fact that Germans still prefer to cook with fresh ingredients, rather than frozen. In fact, your neighbors may head out to a nearby farm on the weekend to buy their eggs or milk, and farmers' markets are very popular.

There is usually a designated shopping area, often in the center of a town or on a long strip in an urban center, offering department stores and larger chain stores. Large-scale indoor and outdoor shopping malls are not as common in Germany. Below are some of the different places you can shop.

Supermarkt (Supermarket)

Supermarkets exist, mostly in cities and larger towns, and are gaining in popularity. Many of them are quite large and sell not only food, but housewares, household items, and even clothing.

Even smaller towns are likely to have a smaller-scale local version of the *Supermarkt*. One such chain of stores is Edeka. These stores usually have a bread counter, a meat counter, locally grown fresh produce, dairy, drinks, magazines, and other kinds of food and necessities one would expect to find in a neighborhood market.

Lebensmittelgeschäft (Grocery Store)

This is your average grocery store, smaller than a *Supermarkt*, but carrying a wide variety of grocery items.

Bäckerei (Bakery)

This is where to go for all kinds of baked goods, from bread to pretzels (German pretzels may well be the best in the world!) to cakes. Many also sell little pizzas, sandwiches, and drinks for the lunch crowd. The *Bäckerei* is usually open quite early so that you can buy your daily bread in time for breakfast.

Metzgerei or Fleischerei (Butcher Shop)

The butcher will be able to sell you all kinds of hot and cold meats, including that American favorite, hamburger. Resist the temptation to "Germanize" the word "hamburger" by using a German accent; a *Hamburger* is someone from the city of Hamburg. Ask the *Metzger* (butcher) for *Rindfleisch* (ground beef) or *gemischtes Gehacktes* (ground pork and beef) instead.

Obst- und Gemüseladen (Fruit and Vegetable Store)

Pretty much what the name suggests, these shops specialize in fruit and veggies, much of it local produce.

Markt (Market)

Most towns have a *Markttag*, or market day, once a week. Check in your local newspaper or with your neighbors to find out the time and location of your local market. If you venture out to the *Marktplatz*, the market place, usually in the city center, you will be able to buy fresh produce, meat, flowers, and lots more. A word of caution: don't squeeze, pick up, or otherwise touch the goods—the vendor will select items for you.

Imbiß (Snack Bar)

Usually open later than traditional stores, you can grab a bite to eat here when your refrigerator is empty. These stores sell wurst, hamburgers, french fries, and other snack food.

Drogerie (Drugstore)

German drugstores, unlike those in the United States, do not include dispensing pharmacies. This is where you can purchase personal hygiene items, cosmetics, candy, and other products.

Apotheke (Pharmacy)

This is where you will get your prescriptions filled and find over-the-counter medications such as aspirin, cold and stomachache remedies, vitamins, and special shampoos. Many *Apotheken* also carry homeopathic, holistic, or whole health products. Germany has different products that are available without prescription, so consider visiting the *Apotheke* for common or minor illnesses. Feel free to ask the pharmacist to recommend a product for your ailment, but don't be surprised if he or she gives you something you're not familiar with, like *Kohletabletten* (charcoal tablets) for an upset stomach! In case you need a prescription filled in an emergency outside of the pharmacy hours, local pharmacies rotate being on call; you should be able to find out who is on call from a listing in your local newspaper or from a sign in any pharmacy's window.

By the Way

MEASURING UP

If you take your favorite recipes with you to Germany, make sure you take your measuring equipment as well! German recipes call for ingredients by weight, not volume. A cake recipe might call for 140 grams of flour. If you'll be following a German recipe, you will need a scale, or you can buy a measuring cup that has markings for the most common ingredients, such as flour or sugar. Note too that if you do pick up an English-language cookbook in Germany, it may have been printed in Britain, and British and American measurements differ somewhat. For example, the British imperial pint, is 20 fluid ounces, while the American pint is only 16 fluid ounces. Even the amount in a tablespoon is different, so be sure you determine which measurements are being used.

SALES, TAX, AND RETURNS

You won't find stores advertising a sale every other weekend as you do in the United States. German shops have two two-week sales per year: one at the end of January/beginning of February (*Winterschlußverkauf,* or winter closeout sale) and one at the end of July/beginning of August (*Sommerschlußverkauf,* or summer closeout sale). However, stores can offer a special price (*Sonderpreis*) on individual items at other times.

Most Americans find at least one benefit to shopping in Germany: sales tax is included in the price. The price you see on the tag is the price you pay. However, the sales tax that you are paying does include VAT, or value-added tax. If you are planning on bringing any of your purchases home with you or sending gifts outside of Germany, you are entitled to a refund of the VAT.

Before you buy, tell the salesperson that you are taking the goods to a non-European country. You will receive an export form or a tax-free shopping check. At your departure, you have to show these forms together with your passport, as well the actual purchase, to a customs official, who documents the export. Remember that your right to a refund expires three months after your purchase. The export forms then have to be sent to the place of purchase, or, if you received a tax-free shopping check, you may cash it in at the Tax Free Shopping Service Center located in most airports. You can also send the checks to the address on the back of the check. Please don't forget to include your account or credit card number.

If you are unable to obtain the necessary stamp on the VAT refund form when leaving Germany, you may obtain it at a German embassy or a consulate. The items purchased must be shown to an official, accompanied by the sales slips, tax forms, and your passport. You will be refunded 16% of your net purchase.

Buying something only to return it to the store is not uncommon in the United States, where you can return everything from a pair of shoes to a diamond necklace and receive a refund, or at least a store credit. This is not the case in Germany, so you'll need to change your mindset before pulling out your wallet. If you buy a pair of chartreuse shoes to wear with an outfit, only to find that the shade isn't quite right, you have nevertheless added the shoes to your permanent collection; the store is not going to take them back. So be very sure you want to keep something before buying it.

The exception to this, of course, is if you end up with a defective product. If the coffeemaker doesn't work, it can be replaced (but not refunded). Don't be surprised if you encounter some suspicion from the salesperson who handles the exchange, however; Germans pride themselves on the quality of their products, so you may get the impression that you are being held accountable for the problem.

Service with a smile is not a well-known concept in Germany, and the customer is not necessarily king. Sales and restaurant service are careers, and salespeople and waitpeople generally take their jobs very seriously and expect to be treated with respect.

If you walk into a shop, it is polite to greet the person behind the counter (probably the owner in a small store) with *Guten Tag*. Don't, however, expect to be approached by a salesperson eager to help you. You may have to seek out someone should you desire assistance.

In many small shops, such as the baker's or butcher's, you probably won't find a well-defined queue. Take note of who was at the counter before you and be prepared to sing out when it is your turn for service. And rest assured that other customers won't hesitate to let you know if you butt in ahead of them!

Americans who relocate to Germany find that they really have to plan their shopping. No more going to the 24-hour supermarket at 10:00 at night to do your shopping. Germany has restricted shopping hours, even in big cities. Almost all retail stores must close by 6:30 during the week, and many smaller stores close for a *Mittagspause* (lunch break) around lunch time. Here are a few tips to plan your shopping:

- Stores are open until 2:00 on Saturday and until 6:00 the first Saturday of every month. A bill to further extend shopping hours was passed by the *Bundestag* in June 2000.
- Many larger cities permit stores to remain open on Thursday until 8:30 PM.
- Stores are closed on Sunday and legal holidays, both federal and local (which are numerous in some states).
- Bakeries can open for three hours on Sunday.
- If you are desperate for milk or juice, or if you forgot to pick up a bottle of wine or flowers to take to the friends who invited you over on a Saturday night, you can try a 24-hour gas station, where you will be able to find the bare necessities (expect to pay for the convenience), or a large train station or airport, assuming there is one in the vicinity, where shops might be open 24 hours. Try to do a bit of reconnaissance work in your

neighborhood when you first arrive so you will know where to go in an emergency.

- Stores are permitted to be open until 6:00 on the four Saturdays preceding Christmas.

BYOB (Bring Your Own Bag) And Other Notes

Newcomers to Germany will notice a few quirks in the German shopping process. Here are some things to keep in mind:

- Many Germans make infrequent car trips to the supermarket for their heavy shopping to load up on essentials, frozen goods, etc. Most daily shopping is done on foot. People carry net or cloth bags for toting their purchases.
- Shopping in Germany is BYOB: bring your own bag. You will be well advised to find a suitable bag or two for your shopping trips. If you don't have a bag, you will have to buy a plastic bag in the store. Purchasing a plastic bag is not for the faint-hearted; you must be prepared to be the recipient of frosty glares, since you are not being environmentally conscious.
- German grocery stores are strictly bag-your-own.
- Clothing stores do provide bags.
- Money should be placed in the small dish that is at every cash register. The cashier won't hold out her hand to receive payment, and you shouldn't hold yours out for your change.

WEIGHTS, MEASURES, AND THE LIKE

Germany uses the metric system of weights and measures. You will have to adjust to reading the temperature in Celsius, figuring distances in kilometers, and buying meat in kilograms. If you're bringing some favorite recipes, don't forget to bring your own measuring cups and spoons, because your German measuring cup will be marked off by weight, not volume. And beware of the German word *Pfund* ("pound"), which is half a kilo or 500 grams. However, the German *Pfund* was officially eliminated several decades ago. (See Appendix C for more information.)

European clothing and shoe sizes are very different from those used in the United States. Although you can say that a woman's size 10 dress is about a 42 in Germany, that is an approximation rather than a rule. As is usually the case, it's best to try a variety of items to get an idea of the sizes that best fit you. (See Appendix C for information on clothing and shoe sizes.)

APPLIANCES AND HOUSEHOLD ITEMS

American appliances do not work in Germany, where 220 volts and 50 hertz are used instead of the 110 volts and 60 hertz used in the United States. In addition, the plugs have two round prongs, not flat ones, so your plug won't fit in the outlet anyway. You can buy an adapter to fit into German outlets, but your appliance still may not be compatible with the voltage. Some appliances have a built-in voltage converter, or you can purchase one. Even with these, you run the risk of blowing a fuse. The 50-hertz system means that your clock, stereo, TV, and VCR, among other things, probably won't work correctly.

Given the problems associated with taking appliances overseas, it is often more practical to budget for buying appliances once you arrive, or to purchase them from an international relocation firm specializing in appliances. Just buying the necessary adapters and converters might cost more than your hairdryer or electric shaver anyway!

You will be able to find all of the modern conveniences one could ask for in Germany. Microwaves are very popular, and frozen foods have become widely available, including frozen dinners, which are popular with single people. You can now even find frozen chocolate-chip cookie dough if you look hard enough! While the typical German mother probably wouldn't consider serving a frozen dinner to the family, she is quite willing to have a side of frozen veggies. (A peek in the window of a German home at dinnertime would convince you that the kitchen remains largely the domain of the woman of the house, even if she is rushing home from work in a business suit. Women who hate cooking can take heart, however: "traditional" family roles are evolving, albeit slowly.)

German refrigerators, although full size, are on the small end of the range of standard sizes. In fact, an immense double-door refrigerator of the type that has become popular in the United States probably wouldn't fit comfortably in a typical German kitchen. Most people in Germany go to the supermarket infrequently to stock up on certain items, but otherwise shop almost daily for fresh food for their daily meals. This reduces the need for refrigerator space. If more space is needed, larger families might have a second refrigerator in the basement for freezing and storing.

Germany, like most of the rest of Europe, uses the PAL video system, not NTSC, which is used in the United States. If you want to take any of your favorite videotapes with you, you'll need to have them converted to PAL, unless you have a multi-system video recorder.

One thing that newcomers to Germany should be aware of is that televisions and radios must be registered. There is a small annual fee that must be paid for each television or radio. Registration is through the *Gebühreneinzugszentrale* (free payment office) (GEZ); you can pick up the registration form at the GEZ or at the post office.

TELEPHONE SERVICE

Telephone service in Germany was a state monopoly until recently. Originally part of the German post office, Deutsche Telekom was spun off and privatized in 1995. Deutsche Telekom lost its monopoly in 1998, when the industry was opened to competition.

Because Deutsche Telekom still controls the phone lines into buildings, you have to arrange your initial telephone service (installation of a new line, if necessary, or the taking over of an existing line) with your local Telekom office. Thereafter, you are free to choose your telephone service provider.

Reduced local rates are rare, but you can shop around for the best long-distance rates, both within Germany and internationally. You do not have to choose a long-distance provider as you do in the United States. You can take advantage of the best rates from any company on a call-by-call basis. Each of the telephone companies has a prefix that you dial before dialing the telephone number to access their services. Calls through those companies then appear on your regular phone bill. Many long-distance providers require that you register before you are able to use their services; this can generally be done with a quick phone call at no addional charge.

American and other non-German telephones do not work in Germany, so don't bother to pack yours. It's quite easy to pick one up once you arrive, either at the Deutsche Telekom shop or from one of the many department stores.

Modems and computers generally work, assuming they have the proper voltage converter, but check with the manufacturer of your hardware to confirm this for your model. Germany offers easy, but expensive, access to the Internet, although prices are dropping rapidly. You will probably want to explore the option of flat-rate Internet access, now offered by some Internet service providers (ISP). When you select an ISP, you will want to know the details of their service. Some offer unlimited access, but you will have to pay per minute for your connect time. However, a few companies now offer a flat-rate package that allows you to dial in to a toll-free number, eliminating the dial-in telephone fees. You choose your Internet service provider from many international (America Online, CompuServe, etc.) or local companies (such as Surfı).

Many new services have recently become available, although most Germans have been slow to use them. These services include caller ID, conference calling, call waiting, call forwarding, and voice mail. To date, many German households (and even many business-es) do not have voice mail or an answering machine. In addition to not being able to leave a message for friends and acquaintances, you may also find that people are not comfortable leaving a message on your machine.

When new telephone books are issued, you will receive a card as a reminder. Take the card with you when you go to pick up your new books. When you first arrive in Germany, you can go to the post office, tell them that you are a new arrival, and pick up a current copy of the yellow and white pages.

Telephone Tips

Here are some practical pieces of information to put you in touch with German telephones, both public and private.

- Public phones using coins are being phased out in favor of *Telefonkarte* (phone card) phones. Many public phones accept only cards. You can purchase a *Telefonkarte* at the post office, *Telefonläden* (telephone shops), *Tabakläden* (tabacco shop), and some stationery stores. Vending machines that sell telephone cards can be found at the *Hauptbahnhof* (main train station) and in some supermarkets. The cards come in 3 EUR, 5 EUR, and 10 EUR denominations.
- Handys (cell phones) are very popular in Germany. However, most American cell phones (and their calling plans) do not work in Germany. Check with your provider prior to your trip to see if your phone will work abroad.
- Phones are also available at the post office for local, national, and international calls. Simply go the counter to be assigned a booth, go to the booth and make your call, then return to the counter to pay your charges (note that there will be a sur-charge). For international calls, go to the counter marked *Auslandsgespräche* (international calls) and follow the same procedure.
- Telephone calls, even local ones, are charged by time units, based on the time of day and the distance you are calling.
- German cities have both a *Fernsprechbuch* (residential directory) and *Gelbe Seiten* (yellow pages).
- Avoid making calls from hotels or restaurants. The surcharge is usually extremely high.
- The main post office might have phone books for other cities as well. However, you can call 11833 for domestic information

and 11834 for international information; there is a small fee when you call either.

- Germans answer their phones with their last name or their telephone number. As the caller, you should always identify yourself in the first few words: *Guten Tag, hier spricht Mary...*
- One should generally not call a German household after 10:00 PM, unless invited to do so.

PETS

Germans love pets, and dogs especially. Don't be surprised if you see dogs in stores and shops or in restaurants and bars. The regulations for bringing pets into the country are vast and complex, depending on the type of animal and the country of origin. If you

would like to bring over your pet, contact the German consulate or embassy well in advance to find out what papers your pet needs and whether or not there is a quarantine or other procedure that applies to your individual case. Once you are there, you will easily be able to find a veterinarian (*Tierarzt*) to take care of your pet's health needs.

If you have a dog, you will need to check at the local town hall about registering it. Most cities require an annual registration fee for dogs (*Hundesteuer*), the amount of which varies from city to city. You will need to keep your dog on a leash in most public places; some dogs might also require a muzzle to discourage fighting. And if you are from a place that doesn't require you to clean up after your dog, you had better get used to it, because you will be expected to do so in Germany.

FINANCIAL MATTERS

Barkauf ist Sparkauf!
Paying with cash is thrifty.

Germany has an excellent, well-organized banking system. Only a small percentage of German banks are publicly owned; most are owned by the governments of the individual states. The Deutsche Bundesbank is the central bank (similar to the Federal Reserve Bank), issuing currency, controlling monetary policy, and performing intermediary financial services.

Germany is a member of the European Union, which has adopted the euro as its currency. Twelve countries have tied their currency together in one exchange rate based on the EMU. In 2002, the EU began to issue euro notes and coins; at that time, the Deutsche Mark was removed from circulation. The euro is now the only accepted currency in Germany, although Deutsche Marks can still be exchanged for euros at banks for a small fee. Coins can no longer be exchanged.

Personal Banking

There are several types of financial institutions, including private banks (Deutsche Bank, Dresdner Bank, and Commerzbank are the largest), savings banks (*Sparkassen*), credit unions (*Genossenschaften*), and even the *Postbank*, which was formerly a part of the post office. All offer similar basic services, such as checking and saving accounts. If you are in the market for more services, such as investing, check to be sure the service is available.

Opening a bank account is a breeze. All you need is your passport for identification and an initial deposit. Although this deposit can be a check written on your account at home, the check can take a while to clear. Cash, of course, will be available to you immediately.

There are two basic types of accounts: the *Sparkonto* (savings account) and the *Girokonto* (revolving or checking account). More people in Germany have savings accounts than in the United States. There is a government restriction on the amount of funds that can be withdrawn in one month from a *Sparkonto*. Additionally, if you want to withdraw the entire amount from a savings account, you must give the bank three months' notice.

The *Girokonto* (or *Giro*) is what most people use for day-to-day banking, such as withdrawing cash and paying bills. Most Germans receive their paycheck through direct deposit to this account. The entire balance of this account is available to you at all times. Your *Giro* automatically comes with a limited overdraft feature. Be careful, though, because there is likely to be interest charged for this "loan."

Upon opening a *Giro*, you will receive a book of Eurochecks and a Eurocard. The Eurocard acts both as an ID for using Eurochecks and as a debit card.

There will probably be monthly fees for both a *Girokonto* and a *Sparkonto*, or a minimum balance that must be maintained; be sure to check with the financial institution for complete information.

Expatriates also have the option of maintaining a special expatriate account at an American bank (such as Citibank) or other international bank (such as Barclays). These accounts are geared toward expatriate needs and can include services such as the payment of your mortgage and other bills "back home," fund transfers, etc. Don't assume, however, that just because you spot a Citibank when you arrive in Düsseldorf they will let you maintain your current account as is; in most cases you cannot make a deposit to a regular American bank account in Germany.

If you will be maintaining both a German and a home account and transferring funds between the two, make sure you do your homework first. While international transfers are fairly standard, they are generally more difficult for smaller banks, and therefore take longer. In addition, there are usually hefty fees applied to international transfers. Be sure that your bank can handle the type of service you need and allow extra time for possible glitches when you are moving funds internationally.

Paying the Bills

In Germany, most people do not pay their monthly bills by check. Instead they use bank transfers for bill paying. There are many ways to do this, depending on the nature of the bill. For regular payments that are the same amount each time, such as the rent, there is the *Dauerauftrag* (standing order). For regular payments in variable amounts, such as the phone or utility bill, there is the *Lastschriftverfahren* (direct debit). Finally, for one-time transfers, such as paying the contractor who put in your kitchen cabinets or put a new roof on your house, there is the *Überweisung* (transfer). Forms for all of these can be obtained at the bank. You simply fill in the relevant information, such as your account number, the payee's account number (this information appears on most bills and invoices), the amount, and the frequency. Your bank statement will list the transfers, and you have the right to dispute the charges up to 90 days after they occur. A word of warning, though: disputed charges are still considered unpaid and may have some unpleasant side effects, such as the discontinuation of your utilities. If you want to dispute a charge, you should contact the billing company to arrange for correct payment as soon as possible.

Credit Cards, Debit Cards, Checks, and ATMs

Germany remains a cash-driven society. You will need to get used to using cash in more situations. The local grocery store in small towns probably won't accept either a credit card or a check, as is common in the United States. Germans in general are leery of using credit, preferring to use cash if they have it and save up for the purchase if they haven't got the funds on hand.

Check use is highly uncommon. You might want to use a check for a large purchase (if, for example, you buy a roomful of furniture), and they are handy if you will be traveling to other European countries, since you can make the check out in the local currency. However, Germans prefer to use a debit card (*Überweisung*) rather than a check. The *Euroscheck* is not a personal bank check but rather similar to a traveler's check. The average German doesn't use personal bank checks at all.

Credit cards are widely accepted in cities, but compared to the United States, not as many Germans have credit cards, and those who do usually have only one card, while Americans average about five. A credit card in Germany does not usually give you the option to pay the balance in installments. The bill has to be paid in full. You may not be able to find a shop that accepts credit cards in very small towns. Most restaurants and shops in cities accept the major credit cards (Visa, MasterCard/Eurocard, American Express).

Debit cards are more popular than credit cards. They have the benefit of acting like cash (satisfying the credit-aversion characteristic) and can be used throughout Europe. While you can't expect to use the card itself in a store, you will easily find a *Geldautomat* (ATM) in most cities. Your debit card will probably work at any machine in Germany; most banks are members of the EC system. But your bank may charge a fee for using the *Geldautomat* at a different bank.

Many, but not all, American debit and credit cards will work at a *Geldautomat*. Cards on the Cirrus and Plus systems will have the best luck, as will Visa cards, but even those are not accepted at every machine. You will receive German marks (or euros), and the amount will be deducted at an exchange rate and service fee according to your bank's policy.

Using Credit

Germans in the past have preferred to save their money and purchase an item outright rather than buy on credit. This extends even to major purchase such as a home. Adult children might live at home for several years until they are able to afford to purchase a house.

More and more, loans are becoming popular for purchasing large-ticket items, such as a car or a mortgage, or to start a small business. Banks are beginning to advertise their "new" loan services, called *Kredit*. However, Germans remain somewhat wary of credit and are far less likely to apply for credit than Americans.

Here, by way of a summary, are some important points to keep in mind when it comes to money and banking in Germany.

- Credit cards are accepted in hotels and most shops, and in airports and train stations. However, don't assume that you can use your credit card as freely as in the United States. Smaller restaurants often don't accept credit cards.
- Since Eurocard is the same as MasterCard, you can use your American MasterCard everywhere you see the Eurocard sign.
- You can probably use your American debit or credit card in ATMs (*Geldautomaten*) in Germany. The Cirrus and Plus systems are the most common, along with Visa. Fees and exchange rates are assessed according to bank policy and vary accordingly.
- Most banks are open Monday through Friday from 8:30 or 9:00 to 4:00; many stay open until 5:30 on Thursday. Smaller branches may close from 1:00 until 2:30 for lunch. Banks are not open on Saturday.
- You can exchange currency or cash traveler's checks in almost any bank. You can also use the currency exchange facilities at airports and major train stations.

SOCIALIZING

Meeting People And Making Friends

One of the hardest parts about moving is reestablishing your social network. When the move is to a new country you often have to find new channels to make friends and to socialize.

Germans and Americans have essentially opposite approaches to establishing friendships. Americans are generally a friendly folk from the outset. Germans who meet Americans for the first time are usually impressed by their openness to new acquaintances, who become instant "friends." However, the German quickly finds out that there are boundaries beneath the surface of the friendship and that most "friendships" are really merely pleasant surface relationships. Americans have many acquaintances (who are called "friends" because "acquaintances" seems too cold) and a few close friends.

When an American arrives in Germany, however, he or she often finds it more difficult to establish friendships. This is not because the Germans are an unfriendly lot, but because they prefer on the whole to maintain a certain distance and reserve until they have had the time to get to know the other person very well. *Bekannte* (acquaintance) is a perfectly acceptable concept in Germany, so most Germans have many *Bekannten* and a few *Freunde* (friends). Because the Germans have taken a long time to get to know one another, the friendship is a deep, lasting one. An American friendship plants annuals that bloom beautifully and riotously, but can fade after a time; a German friendship plants a bonsai, which must be carefully shaped, but which will last a lifetime.

So how do you go about making German friends? The best way is to do the things you like to do. If you have kids or a dog you like to take to the park, visit a nearby park (there is bound to be one; Germany is a very "green" country) where you can meet other parents or dog lovers. Go hiking, play chess, go to a lecture on ancient Chinese history—whatever interests you. Germans are great joiners. For any activity that your imagination conjures up, there is sure to be

a club or organized group nearby. To find a group that you might like to join, check at the tourist office, in the telephone book or local newspaper, or ask around at work. Go to the places people with your interests might gather or exchange information, like the library to find a book discussion group or an outdoor outfitter to find people who like to camp.

Most of all, realize that it can take much longer to form a friendship with a German than with a fellow American. But if you are willing to invest the time, the friendship will be a rewarding, lifelong one.

Be My Guest: Being on Your Best Behavior as a Host or Guest

We all tend to display our better manners when we are guests or when we have them. The German tradition is to have a male host and a female hostess. In the most formal of occasions, a single person would ask a person of the opposite gender to share the hosting duties. As elsewhere, times change. Therefore, the following suggestions use the word "host" to cover both genders in most cases; you can decide what is appropriate in your own situation.

An invitation to a home is a special privilege and should be accompanied by a small gift, such as wine (probably the most popular), flowers, chocolates, a small fruit basket, or a small trinket reflecting one's home culture. Even when popping by someone's house for coffee, most guests will bring a small coffee cake or other treat. If you decide to bring flowers, make it an uneven number, but not thirteen. If the flowers are wrapped in paper, unwrap them before presenting them. (Because most people unwrap the flowers while standing on the doorstep, your German host will probably hold out one hand for the flowers and one for the discarded wrapping.) Certain flowers hold special significance: red roses (love), carnations (mourning), yellow or white chrysanthemums or calla lilies (funerals). A mixed bouquet is always appropriate, and always a safe choice! If you are unsure, you can tell the florist what the occasion is and ask for advice.

If a dinner party is the reason for your visit, and if there is a female guest of honor, she is seated next to the host; the male guest of honor sits next to the hostess. Couples are not seated next to each other; after all, you talk to each other all the time, so it will be more interesting to mix people up. The host will indicate that guests should begin eating by saying *Guten Appetit*. Remember that it is impolite to drink before your host does.

Don't expect to stay around for a long time after dinner. Your hosts won't rush you out the door; as the guest it's up to you to leave before overstaying your welcome. If the party was in honor of someone, that person should initiate the leavetaking, followed closely by other guests.

If you are entertained in someone's home, don't ask to be shown around. You are not likely to see anything except the living room and the dining room while you are there. While you can certainly compliment your hosts on their home or furnishings, make sure your comments are sincere and low-key, not merely fulsome praise. Excessive praise is inappropriate and tends to ring hollow.

Your host will invite you to have a seat or to mingle if it is a larger party. It's the host's duty to make sure his or her guests become acquainted if they don't know one another. At very large parties you may need to introduce yourself to people; otherwise you can probably expect your host to take you on an introductory tour of the room to make you feel more comfortable. Drinks will be offered soon after you arrive; expect to be served by your host rather than being told to "go get yourself a drink."

Don't help yourself to your host's refrigerator or kitchen; wait to be offered food or drink. Incidentally, the door to a German bathroom stays closed, even when unoccupied. Knock before entering and close the door behind you when you leave. Ask for the *Toilette* (toilet), not the "restroom" or "bathroom," which have different meanings.

It is appropriate to send a simple thank-you note or call your host with thanks following your visit.

Socializing Tips and Tidbits

- German women usually prefer a handshake upon introduction. Men should wait for the woman to extend her hand first. Women who know each other well may kiss each other's cheek in greeting in social situations.
- Germans prefer to call ahead instead of just dropping by a friend's house. However, if you mention to a friend she should "stop by sometime," don't be surprised if she shows up on your doorstep without warning; this kind of social nicety is not common in Germany, and she may have taken your words literally.
- Try not to arrive at someone's house empty-handed. Even if you are going over to a friend's house just for coffee and conversation, take along a small treat, such as a coffee cake or some cookies.

ETIQUETTE

While an etiquette faux pas might not cause a war to break out, continually ignoring how things are done locally in favor of how you used to do them at home is a sure sign of disrespect. Faux pas are overlooked; rudeness is not.

Communicating

Reden ist Silber, Schweigen ist Gold.
Speech is silver, silence is golden.

Germans do not use first names as freely as Americans. Address people by their courtesy titles (*Herr/Frau*), academic titles (*Herr/Frau Doktor*), or professional titles (*Herr/Frau Direktor*). Use last names unless invited to do otherwise. This is particularly true in business situations. Don't expect to be invited to use first names; it is not a personal slight, as they will also use your last name. When introducing someone, be sure to include his or her last name plus title (*Herr Schmidt* or *Frau Doktor Müller*). In informal situations among young people, use of first names is common. Observe what other people are doing and follow suit.

English is widely spoken. However, it can be offensive if you make that assumption and begin speaking in English. Speak a few words of German first, if you can, even if it's only a greeting, then ask if the person minds if you continue in English. If you don't know any German, the language section and accompanying CD at the back of this book will get the ball rolling for you. Never underestimate the value of knowing even a few simple phrases and expressions. If you do speak some German, be sure to maintain proper formality with your use of *Sie* (formal "you") and *du* (informal "you"); when in doubt, use *Sie*.

The best conversational openers are general topics, such as compliments about the country or city, sports, arts, music, etc. Germans

are uncomfortable being asked personal questions by people they've just met; avoid questions about family, spouses, education, personal finances, or religious affiliation. It's fine to ask questions or discuss cultural differences, but avoid criticism. Put yourself in the other person's shoes and think about how you would react to hearing negative comments about your country or the way you do things.

In the eyes of Americans, Germans tend to appear straightforward and direct. They say what they are thinking, and spend little time on small talk. To an American ear, German intonation may make the speaker seem aggressive or angry, even when he or she is not. This is just a linguistic difference; don't read into it or judge it by the standards you apply to American English.

Most Germans love a good debate or discussion. This tends to put off most Americans, who prefer to avoid conflict in conversation. These discussions require you to state your opinion intelligently and logically and not take a differing opinion as a personal attack. Remember that in any verbal exchange, eye contact is used to signal interest, attention, and comprehension. Maintain it!

By the Way...

A TOKEN GESTURE

Germans as a rule are not as well known for gesticulation as other Europeans. Most of the gestures you use at home will be mutually understood. There are, however, a few noteworthy differences.

Germans don't cross their fingers for luck; they press their thumbs. There is both a spoken expression of luck (den Daumen drücken, to "press one's thumbs"), as in "I'll cross my fingers for you," and a gesture, where you make a fist with thumb inside. The meaning is the same. If you go the route of the gesture, though, be sure you don't let your thumb stick out between your first and second fingers; this is obscene!

To indicate that someone is crazy, Germans tap their forehead or temple with their index finger. Don't be surprised if you are the recipient of this gesture if you're driving in the left lane on the Autobahn when another driver goes roaring past!

Germans often rap on the table or arm of the chair in lieu of applause. This is more commonly heard in a lecture hall or a conference room than at a cultural event, where one does applaud.

And last but not least, if you're in a bar and hold up your index finger (to mean "one") to ask for another, you may well get two more, especially if you're not alone. Germans begin counting with their thumbs, so the index finger is associated with the number two, not the number one.

GIFTS

Social gift giving is popular, but not expected, except for host/hostess gifts. While there are no hard and fast rules for social gift giving, Germans tend to exchange gifts (at Christmas, birthdays, etc.) only with close friends. Casual friends might go out for a drink or drop by the house for coffee and cake (bringing a bottle of wine!) as a way of expressing celebration.

ENTERTAINMENT

The German heritage is marked by high culture. German theater, concerts, and operas are among the best in Europe. Opportunities for entertainment abound, from an evening at the local *Kneipe* (pub) to a night at the ballet. Tickets to most performances are available through the local tourist information office, as well as at the venue's box office.

Cinemas are popular, although most movies are dubbed into German rather than subtitled. Discos, cafés, and pubs are also well attended, especially since there are no designated closing times for these. Germans enjoy an evening at the local beer garden for a get-together with friends.

Contemporary popular music can be heard in local bars, beer halls, beer gardens and small arenas. Jazz is big in Germany, and the larger cities have jazz clubs. And if you like sports, you've come to the right place. *Fußball* (soccer) is taken very seriously, especially at World Cup time; skiing and tennis are also popular. If you want to participate instead of just watching, you will probably find a club for your favorite sport nearby. In fact, you can find a club for virtually anything you like to do, from hiking to chess to table tennis.

Dating and Beyond

If you are a single person moving to Germany, or if you have teenagers, you probably have some questions about dating. Dating rituals are quite similar to those in the United States. First dates usually take place in a nice restaurant or café, not in the local dive. Subsequent dates could be any number of things from a movie to a picnic. In the initial stages of a romantic relationship, most Germans favor the traditional approach of the gentleman paying for the activities. However, depending on the financial status of the individuals, both may contribute in later stages.

Teenage socializing and dating are also similar to that of American teenagers. Teens tend to congregate and socialize in groups. You will have to start worrying about your child dating at approximately the same time—in the mid- or even early teens.

For both adults and teens, holding hands and walking arm in arm in public are perfectly acceptable. However, more overt or lewd displays in public, such as extended kissing, are not common.

While dating rituals are similar in Germany and the United States, attitudes toward sex are not. Generally speaking, Americans remain somewhat puritanical about sex. Sex has a mystery and near-taboo about it that has become very powerful; it is probably the number one tool for selling consumer goods in the United States.

In Germany, attitudes toward sex are much more relaxed. Whereas the United States tends to censor sex and allow violence in movies, television, etc., Germany censors violence and allows sex. Many popular publications include pictures that would be considered pornographic in the United States, even though they are in reality merely nudity, not depictions of sexual nudity. Late-night television, commercials, and magazines routinely show topless women (and sometimes nude men, although not as frequently). Germany's sex industry is much more open than that of the United States. Magazines with sexual content can be purchased at most magazine stands by people as young as twelve. Prostitution is legal, and most cities have a "red light district" where sex is a commercial service.

Children are exposed to nudity at a very young age, but because of the more open environment, sex is treated as something natural, not something forbidden. Accordingly, German teens tend to be much more mature about sex than their American counterparts. This can be quite an adjustment for American children, especially teens, who are on the cusp of sexual maturity.

It follows, then, that sex before marriage is nothing to be remarked on. Birth control is readily available, from condoms at the local drug store to prescription contraceptives. Condom vending machines are found in the restrooms of most gas stations, discos, and clubs.

If you are engaged to a German national and will be married in Germany, start planning well ahead of time, as there is a considerable amount of red tape that must be taken care of first. You can check with a nearby embassy or consulate for information on the necessary forms and documentation. A marriage in Germany is a civil ceremony that takes place at the *Standesamt* (magistrate's office). A religious ceremony following the civil ceremony is optional, and most Germans do not have one.

By the Way...

MAY-DECEMBER ROMANCES

Your German girlfriend or boyfriend writes to you to say that she or he will be arriving at the airport on 12/5. Well, that's really advance notice, you think, since it's just the middle of April, but what the heck. You mark it in your planner for December 5. Not so fast. That's actually May 12. Remember that Germans write the day first and then the month, so 12/5 is the 12th day of May. Lucky for you if you figure this out in time and are there at the airport with flowers and chocolates.

Homosexuality

Gays in Germany, as in many countries, find that larger cities offer a more open and friendly environment. In most smaller towns it is not acceptable to be openly gay, and many people have left their home towns for this reason. Many large cities have a "gay" neighborhood, such as the St. Pauli section of Hamburg, which has gay bars, shows, etc.

Being openly gay in your personal life is an individual choice. Being openly gay in the workplace, however, is more complex. For one thing, there is no place in most professional relationships for that kind of personal information, regardless of sexual preference. For the most part, there is no reason for the topic to come up. As a rule, conservatism in both dress and conduct is expected in German business for everyone. Even industries that are considered less conservative, such as advertising, have not reached the point that the open expression of one's sexual preference is acceptable in the workplace.

FOOD

As a rule, German food is fresh and of high quality. Pork is the main meat source in the German diet. Vegetarians, especially those following a vegan diet, will probably find that their options are limited when going to a restaurant; vegetarian restaurants are not always easy to find. Many people think of German cuisine as the stereotypical sausage-and-sauerkraut, but you will be doing your palette a disservice if you insist on such narrow thinking. The German is, in fact, as sophisticated a diner as you will find anywhere in the world. In addition to fantastic traditional dishes such as wurst (yes, the Germans are the world's *Wurstmeisters*, making dozens of varieties of sausage), *Sauerbraten,* and *Gulasch,* you will be able to try all manner of game, from venison to boar and from quail to duck, as well as seafood (especially along the coasts of the Baltic and North seas) and many other dishes.

The bakery's shelves are laden with a wide variety of choices, such as rye, pumpernickel, and multi-grain breads. Your waistline is liable to expand just by looking at the confections of chocolate, marzipan, cream, and honey. Germany's Alpen Allgäu region is the place to find cheeses such as Limburger and Emmenthaler.

Germany is renowned for its beer, which is truly superb, but not many people are familiar with Germany's quality wines. *Riesling* is probably the best known of the German wines, but there are many types to choose from. Wine aficionados can find plenty of information about German wines at a local bookstore or on the Internet—a good place to start is the official site of the German Wine Information Bureau at www.germanwineusa.org. Beer-lovers probably already know that there are over 1,500 breweries in Germany. If you find yourself traveling through a small town, stop to see if there is a local brewery; some of the best beers aren't found in the store! If you like beer but aren't familiar with German beer, the most common types are *helles* (light, referring to color, not caloric content), *dunkles* (dark), Pilsner, and *Weizen* (or *Hefeweizen*). Each has a very different taste, so you may have to try them all to see which ones appeal to you.

Restaurants, cafes, pizzerias, kebab houses, and fast-food restaurants abound in Germany. Most restaurants display their prices and menus at the door. Many restaurants, especially if they are family owned and operated, are closed one day a week, often on Monday.

Dining Etiquette

Dining manners in Germany are not substantially different from those in the United States. In general, the table manners you learned from your parents will stand you in good stead in Germany: German moms don't let their kids slurp their soup, talk with their mouths full, or belch at the table either. Following are some of the differences you will see. Of course, the best advice about table manners, no matter where in the world you are, is to take things slowly, watch your dining companions, and take your cues from their actions.

Table settings are the same as in the United States, but more religiously adhered to. Here, too, one begins with the outermost utensil. Incidentally, Germans do not often eat with their fingers. Items considered "finger food" in the United States, such as burgers or chicken, are eaten with knife and fork.

A German meal usually begins with drinks. Toasting is quite common. It can range from informal (*Prost, Prosit,* or *zum Wohl*) with friends or a more elaborate speech on formal occasions. If you're at a large gathering, it isn't necessary to throw yourself across the table to touch the glass of your counterparts on the far end, but do clink glasses with everyone within reasonable reach of your glass. Beer is an important part of Germany's cuisine; it is the most common beverage at meals. A German will be flattered at a chance to recommend a tasty beer.

Guten Appetit is said before eating; if there is a host, that's the signal to start eating. The appropriate response is a returned *Guten Appetit* or *Danke, ebenfalls* (Thank you, likewise).

When eating, the knife is held in the right hand, the fork in the

left. Utensils are not switched between hands; hang on to both (unless you are taking a drink, using your spoon, etc.) between bites. Americans tend to cut several pieces of meat or other foods at once, then switch their fork to their right hands. In Germany, since one keeps one's utensils in hand, the tendency is to cut and eat one piece at a time. Basic everyday etiquette also requires that you keep your hands above the table at all times (but your elbows off the table). Although this is contrary to the American impulse to put the hand not holding the fork in one's lap, it's a whole lot easier if you keep your utensils in your hands, as mentioned above. If you're eating fish, you will probably get a fish knife. Be sure to use it instead of the regular knife. Traditional etiquette requires that you not use your knife to cut vegetables, dumplings, etc., as that would suggest that the items are improperly prepared. For soup, tilt your bowl away from you and scoop outward with your spoon.

When not using your utensils during the meal, cross them on your plate, not on the table. Never chew with your mouth open, or speak with food in your mouth. Chewing noises that might go unnoticed in the United States become painfully obvious once you are in Germany.

It is not necessary to leave anything on your plate; doing so could in fact be considered wasteful. When you have finished your meal, place your knife and fork side by side on the right side of your plate, tilted diagonally toward the center. If you are just taking a small break, rest the fork on the left side of the plate with the prongs up and the knife on the right.

Restaurants

Depending on the time of day and what type of food sets your taste buds tingling, you'll find a variety of choices for your dining pleasure. The most sophisticated restaurants, and consequently the most expensive, are found in larger cities, offering haute cuisine to satisfy any appetite. If you're in the market for simpler fare, try a *Gaststätte* (similar to a pub) or *Gasthof* (inn). If you want to grab a quick bite, you will easily find an *Imbiß* in pedestrian and shopping areas, in markets, and in train stations. Cafés, indoor or outdoor, offer the opportunity to sit and relax over a cup of coffee and people-watch. If you absolutely can't live without fast food, you will find McDonald's, Pizza Hut, and other fast-food chains throughout Germany. Restaurants featuring Italian, Chinese, Turkish, Greek, and other national cuisines offer a change of pace.

Restaurants close early by American standards, usually between 9:30 and 10:30 PM. Most are also closed one day a week, typically Monday, Tuesday, or Wednesday. Restaurants are open only for lunch and dinner, and they're closed in between those meals. It's difficult to find a place that serves breakfast. Some cafés offer breakfast, but your choices will probably be bread and cheese or jam, *Müsli*, and perhaps a soft-boiled egg. Hearty "American" breakfasts, with copious amounts of eggs, bacon, sausage, pancakes, and the like, are simply not the norm in Germany, or in most places outside of the United States for that matter.

Reservations are necessary only for more expensive restaurants. If you want to be on the safe side, you can always call to see if you can make a reservation in a more casual restaurant. However, some establishments do not accept reservations. If you arrive at a casual restaurant to find that there are no free tables, you may sit at a table where there is room. Ask the current occupants for permission to sit at their table. When this happens, exchange a brief greeting with your fellow diners. You are not, however, obligated to carry on a conversation with them after that. Please note that this is not acceptable behavior at a more upscale restaurant, where one waits to be seated.

Another curious sight in German restaurants is a patron walking through the door accompanied by a dog. Germans love their pets, and they see no reason why their dogs shouldn't be able to accompany them to a meal out. On the other hand, German parents don't take their children to restaurants as often as American parents do. When children do eat out with their parents, they are expected to be well behaved and closely monitored by their parents, and not disturb other patrons. If you have young kids, check around your neighborhood for places with more child-friendly atmospheres.

If you need to attract the attention of the waiter or waitress, raise your hand. You can add *Herr Ober* (for the waiter) or *Fräulein* (for the waitress) if they don't happen to be looking in your direction. Feel free to ask for assistance when making a decision about what to order. However, don't expect the same latitude for substitutions and special orders ("I'd like to have rice instead of potatoes with that" or "Put the salad dressing on the side") that you have in the United States. Many restaurants have a fixed-price lunch menu (*Tageskarte*) that includes the day's special at a very reasonable price. Of course, you can always order à la carte.

Germans do not drink tap water. The majority of German households have bottled water delivered to them by the case. In a restaurant, then, a request for water will almost always get you a full bottle of mineral water. You can specify plain water (*ohne Kohlensäure*) if you prefer, but it may not be available. Drinks are usually served without ice. Even if you request ice, do not expect the glacier that is the norm in American glasses. You'll probably get only a (small) cube or two. And be prepared to pay for those refills!

When the time comes to pay the bill, just give the money to the waiter or waitress. It is generally understood that the person who issues an invitation to a restaurant also pays for the meal. The guest should then reciprocate at the next get-together, keeping things on an even keel. Separate bills are common, though, in appropriate situations, such as a mutual plan to eat out together. This is the norm when several friends get together or if two couples meet for dinner. Just let the waiter or waitress know in advance so the bill can be calculated correctly. They're accustomed to adding up separate checks, so don't be afraid to ask for one. It is not necessary to gather the appropriate amount from everyone so that the table can pay all at once. The waiter or waitress will collect from each person in turn.

When you're expecting change back, simply tell your waiter how much change to give you. For example, if your bill comes to 10,20 EUR and you give the waiter 15 EUR, you can ask for 4 EUR back, leaving 0,80 EUR in *Trinkgeld* ("drink money," or tip). This is a more common practice than leaving the tip on the table when you leave. Note that service is included in the bill by law in all restaurants. So you can just round up to the nearest mark or add a few extra marks to the bill as an additional tip for the waiter or waitress. And remember that wages for waitstaff are higher than in the United States, so you don't have to feel guilty for leaving only a small tip. In upscale restaurants, however, a tip of about 10% is expected.

HEALTH AND SAFETY

Health

Germany is a wonderfully clean and healthy nation. Your health-care concerns in Germany will be no different from what they are in the

United States. German medical facilities are among the best in the world, with up-to-date equipment and well-trained medical staffs. If you do need medical attention during your stay in Germany, you will be well cared for.

If you are moving to Germany, you must have medical insurance (*Krankenversicherung*). You can choose the national health insurance program, subsidized by the government, or private insurance. Your company probably has a medical insurance program in place, but you will want to find out the details, and you can always choose a different one.

International travelers should consider reviewing their medical-insurance policies, since most policies do not cover medical care outside of the country. Check with your insurance provider to verify what kind of coverage, if any, you will have while you are abroad. You may be able to add a rider for international coverage. If your insurance provider does not offer coverage outside of your home country, there are companies that specialize in insurance for expatriates and international travelers. Your insurance agent should be able to help you select appropriate coverage. Note that no immunizations are required to enter Germany.

If you need a doctor, you will need to have your insurance card handy. You can call your doctor's office to make routine appointments. Clinics and hospital emergency rooms are available for urgent care. If you would prefer to have a doctor come to you, check around for one who makes house calls—they do exist, but you can expect to pay for that convenience.

Unless you speak German, you may be more comfortable with an English-speaking doctor. You can ask friends and colleagues for recommendations or obtain a list from an American embassy or consulate.

If you need medicine or other health-care products (stomachache or cold remedies, aspirin, etc.) you will need to go to an *Apotheke*. Pharmacists are highly qualified. You can feel free to ask them for their recommendation for an over-the-counter product for your particular symptoms. Natural or homeopathic remedies are quite popular and do not require a prescription. Prescriptions for drugs must be obtained from a doctor. However, quite a few medications that require a prescription in the United States are available over the counter in Germany. A chat with your local pharmacist will help you figure out how to get what you need.

Crime

While traveling in Germany, take the same basic precautions taken by savvy travelers everywhere. This list isn't exhaustive, but here are a few important points to keep in mind:

- Don't flash jewelry or camera equipment
- Don't leave baggage or belongings unattended
- Lock your car and put valuables out of sight in the trunk
- Use a money belt
- Always guard your wallet, purse, and passport
- Guard against pickpockets, especially in large cities and crowded situations, such as festivals or markets

You should also make photocopies of important documents, including your driver's license and passport, and keep them in a safe place, separate from the originals.

Violent crime is less common in Germany than in the United States. Muggings and assaults are uncommon. Larger cities tend to see higher crime rates, mostly in house robberies and car theft. If you are the victim of a crime, report it to the police immediately. Keep in mind that drug possession is a serious crime in Germany.

Emergency Numbers

Emergency phone numbers vary somewhat throughout Germany; check your phone book to verify the local number. The police can usually be reached by calling 110, the fire department and ambulance by calling 112.

POST OFFICE

The post office is normally open Monday–Friday from 8:00 AM to 6:00 PM, and Saturday from 9:00 to noon. In smaller towns, the post office may be closed from 1:00 to 3:00 PM. In large cities there may be one post office (often at the train station) that offers 24-hour service. Mail service within Germany is quite efficient. Letters sent within Germany usually arrive on the following day; mail to the United States takes between 5 and 10 business days. You can buy stamps (*Briefmarken*) from machines located outside most post offices and in railway stations. For the stamp collector, *Sondermarken* (commemorative stamps) are available at no additional charge.

Mailboxes are yellow and have the postal horn on them. Blue boxes marked *Luftpost* are for airmail only. German addresses are written as follows:

Name
Schillerstraße 29   (street name, number)
04105 Leipzig   (postal code, city)

From outside Germany, add a D- (for Deutschland) in front of the zip code: D-04105 Leipzig.

Following are some of the delivery services offered by the post office:

Einschreiben	(registered letter)
Rückschein	(return receipt)
Express-Briefe	(special delivery)

In addition to processing mail, most post offices have additional functions. You can make local and long-distance calls from telephones located in the post office, purchase telephone cards, and even do a limited amount of banking there if you have a postal savings account. Radio and television license fee forms are also available at the post office (although you must take them to the GEZ to register). If you will be away from home for an extended period, you will need to set up a post office box to hold your mail.

By the Way...

WHAT TIME IS IT?

You check your *Armbanduhr* (watch) and even glance up at the *Uhrturm* (clock tower). Yup, it's 9:00 all right, and night has fallen. Where the heck is your train? And you thought German trains were supposed to run on schedule. Unfortunately for you, time in Germany is often expressed according to a 24-hour clock, especially for official schedules and the like. Therefore 9:00 is 9:00 AM, not PM, which is 21:00. Your train was there and on time. It left promptly at 9:00, twelve hours ago.

TIPPING

Tipping is often confusing outside of your own culture. You'll find much of this information elsewhere in the applicable sections of this book, but since tipping can be the cause of both frustration and anxiety, here's a simple and practical summary.

Tipping is not as common in Germany as it is in the United States. Service positions, such as waitstaff and taxi drivers, are paid a salary that does not rely on tips to maintain a minimum standard of living. Therefore, most tips tend to be small and are an expression of appreciation for exceptional service.

Here are some general guidelines:

- In a restaurant, service is included in the bill. This is because every price on the menu has to be an end price by law. In upscale restaurants, a 10% tip is common. Round up to the nearest mark or add an extra mark to the bill as an additional tip (*Trinkgeld*) for the waiter/waitress.
- The same applies to taxi drivers. There is generally a small extra charge for luggage, but you can add a bit more if the driver has helped you with the luggage.
- Porters/bellhops are found only in more expensive hotels. One EUR per suitcase is appropriate.
- Doormen are found only at more exclusive hotels; tipping is not necessary.
- If you would like to give the hotel maid a tip, leave the money in an envelope in the room; never give the tip to the maid in person. Some hotels now provide a special envelope for guests who would like to leave a tip. One EUR per night is appropriate if the room was well kept during your stay.
- Many restrooms in Germany have an attendant who cleans the stalls after use and sometime doles out toilet paper. Men will often find a woman attending the men's room. There will be a small dish on a table or on the counter for tips. Tip at least 0,25 EUR.
- If there is a coat check, there may be a small jar for tips. However, tipping is by no means obligatory. Fifty cents is fine.
- Most people leave an envelope for their postal carrier around Christmastime. Ten EUR is an appropriate amount.
- Skycaps don't exist in Germany; baggage handling at the airport is strictly self-service. Coin-operated cart rental is available throughout airports and train stations.
- Maître d's are not tipped.
- Deliverymen are not tipped.

- Food delivery from a few restaurants, such as pizza parlors and Chinese restaurants, does exist. However, the delivery-person is not tipped.
- Bartenders *never* get a tip. Tipping the bartender will most definitely mark you as the American!

SIX

BUSINESS ENVIRONMENT

Before beginning to do business with Germans or in Germany, it will be helpful to learn about the German business environment. This section will acquaint you with the basics of business in Germany.

COMPANY VALUES

Profit is the name of the game for German business. However, German companies—and the German people—place a very high value on quality. These two ideas, profit and quality, make a very neat circle, since the German willingness to pay more for a well made product means that companies can make a profit without sacrificing quality.

When compared to their American counterparts, German companies seem to have more concern for the well-being of their employees. Of course, it is difficult to determine how much is the result of human concern and how much is due in part to legal requirements. In the final analysis, however, it seems that each nurtures the other. A caring environment leads to legislation benefiting employees which in turn perpetuates a positive work environment. Thus the worker enjoys a stable work environment with many benefits, and the company benefits by the creation of a stable work force. Most Germans are proud of and are quite loyal to the company they work for.

GERMAN SERVICE

One frequently-noted difference between Americans and Germans is their respective notion of what "service" means. Most Americans are accustomed to the ideas of "service with a smile" and "the customer is king." Unfortunately, neither of these two slogans appears in the German language. In fact, a German is more likely to complain that American business places are all smiles with no real substance.

Service in Germany has no particular focus on friendliness or pleasantness. Foremost in the German mind is the quality of the item. Germans pride themselves in the extremely high-quality products they bring to the market and few Germans would sacrifice quality for a lower price. Service, therefore, is about providing information about products. Being a salesperson, with all that entails in the American retail environment, is unnecessary in Germany because it is the quality of the product that will influence the consumer, not the personality of the salesperson.

From the American viewpoint, German customer-service representatives and salespeople exhibit behavior that borders on rudeness. Interpreted in the German context, though, it is better characterized as efficiency. German service personnel are not taught to add a spark of personality to their interactions with customers to ensure a "pleasant" encounter, but to provide the customer with the information required.

Companies that have incorporated ideas such as "service with a smile" into their customer-relations priorities have found it challenging to train their German employees to provide this type of service.

COMPANY STRUCTURE

Germany has a variety of legal company structures, ranging from the limited liability of the *Aktiengesellschaft* and the *Gesellschaft mit beschränkter Haftung* to partnerships and branches.

An *Aktiengesellschaft* (AG; stock company) is a joint stock corporation wherein shareholders are not personally liable for the organization's debts. A minimum of five members, individual or corporate, and a minimum share capital of DM 100.000 is required to form an AG. A management board represents the corporation's shareholders.

A *Gesellschaft mit beschränkter Haftung* (GmbH; company with limited liability) is the most common form of business for the subsidiaries of foreign companies in Germany and for family businesses. A GmbH can be formed by a single shareholder with a minimum capital requirement of 25.565 EUR. A GmbH has one or more directors in lieu of a management board; shareholders have direct access to management. An *Aufsichtsrat* (supervisory board) is not necessary for GmbH companies with fewer than 500 regular employees.

There are several types of partnerships, including:

Offene Handelsgesellschaft (OHG). A general partnership wherein all partners have unlimited liability for debts of the partnership.

Kommanditgesellschaft (KG). A limited partnership in which at least one partner has unlimited liability for the partnership's debt; other partners may have limited liability up to the amount of their capital investment.

GmbH & Co Kommanditgesellschaft (GmbH & Co KG). A limited partnership with a GmbH as general partner and individuals as limited partners.

Stille Gesellschaft. A partnership in which an unregistered silent partner contributes capital but leaves the management of the business to the active partner.

In addition, there are also *Genossenschaften* (cooperatives), *Einzelkaufmänner* (sole proprietors), and *Niederlassungen ausländischer Gesellschaften* (branches of foreign companies).

The structure of authority in most German organizations is very hierarchical. In older firms, such as Bosch, the hierarchy is very rigid. This rigid hierarchy, like German business, has its roots in manufacturing, with a large number of workers organized by a small number of managers. Newer businesses, especially those that are service-oriented, are adopting a less hierarchical structure. This is the result of many factors, including the evolution of business from manufacturing to service, the creation of new companies unburdened by a history of hierarchy, and a new generation of managers. However, German businesses in all sectors remain more hierarchical than the typical American business.

THE CHAIN OF COMMAND

German public companies are controlled by two separate boards: the *Aufsichtsrat*, or supervisory board, and the *Vorstand*, or management board. The *Aufsichtsrat* approves major decisions and is responsible for the election and termination of the *Vorstand*. The *Vorstand* is responsible for the firm's day-to-day operations.

The topmost members of the organization make it their business to be informed of any major developments. Decisions on things such as major budget expenditures and new projects must have their stamp of approval. Because there are often two or more people at this level, the flow of decisions can become bottlenecked at the highest levels.

Thanks to the Works Constitution Act of 1972, German employees have a direct say in their company's decision-making. Any business that has five or more non-management employees must have a

Betriebsrat, or Works Council. The *Betriebsrat* consists of representatives elected by the company's employees, and its purpose is to represent the workers' interests to the company. Most *Betriebsrat* representatives take this responsibility on a voluntary basis in addition to their regular duties. Companies with more than 300 employees, however, must have one or more full-time representatives. Similar regulations apply to government and other public organizations as well.

The *Betriebsrat* is charged with myriad responsibilities. For example, it ensures that all laws and regulations, such as those concerning workplace safety, are met. It also sees that wage agreements are kept, and that working hours, holidays, pay structures and job descriptions are respected. The laws regarding the role of the *Betriebsrat* are very exact. For example, in a company with 20 or more employees, management must obtain the approval of the *Betriebsrat* in certain matters such as hiring and company restructuring. If the *Betriebsrat* refuses approval, the matter must be taken before the Labor Court for resolution.

Codetermination is an idea the Germans take very seriously. It ensures that workers can influence company policy and has its foundations in the belief that the democratic process must apply to all sectors, not just to government. In addition to the *Betriebsrat*, employees are represented on the *Aufsichtsrat* (up to 50% of the board members) and have further representation in the form of a labor director. The exact representation of the workers in the company's affairs depends on several things, such as the size and structure of the company and when the company was founded.

COMPARTMENTALIZATION

The German business environment is one of compartmentalization. Each division of the company has its own responsibilities, and each individual within that division has his or her own tasks. The result is something akin to wearing blinders, with departments existing within separate bubbles, often with very little communication between them. While Germans in general are quite efficient, this compartmentalization can lead to breakdowns in efficiency. A good example of this is when someone goes on vacation. Very often that person's responsibilities will simply hang in limbo. If one of his or her clients calls with a question or problem, it is possible that nothing will be resolved until that person returns from vacation.

THE 37-HOUR WORK WEEK AND OTHER BENEFITS

The German work week averages about 37 hours or less in most places. Many offices accomplish this by closing early, between noon and 2:00 PM, on Friday. Unions continually push for fewer hours. Overtime is generally discouraged, and most people leave the office at 5:00.

In addition to one of the world's shortest work weeks, Germans also enjoy a liberal vacation benefit when compared to most countries, as well as 12 to 15 legal holidays, depending on location. Every worker is entitled to a minimum of four weeks of vacation; seniority at an organization will net you up to six weeks. If a holiday falls on a Thursday, the Friday is usually a wash, since most people don't come in for the following half-day.

When you combine all of this with the fact that most Germans prefer to take their vacation days all at one time, you will find that an individual might be out of the office for a month or longer at a time. Popular vacation months include May and June because vacation days can be taken in conjunction with the many legal holidays during these months, maximizing consecutive days off to the hilt. July and August are also popular choices.

German health benefits are substantial as well. Employees are allowed to take a one-week *Kur* (literally, cure), a visit to one of Germany's famous spas or a health resort, once every two years. Should a German employee fall sick, he or she is allotted six weeks of fully paid sick leave, followed by a period in which health insurance pays up to 90% of the employee's salary until recovery or retirement as a result of the health problem.

Maternity and paternity leave are also generous. Mothers-to-be can take six weeks of fully paid leave before the birth of the child and they have eight more weeks of full pay afterward (more for multiple births). The doting dad or mom can take up to three years of unpaid leave to stay at home with the baby, secure in the knowledge that the job will be waiting for them upon their return.

With all of the combined benefits that the German employee enjoys, one of the biggest complaints from Americans is that the person they need seems to be constantly away from the office. When you put that together with the time difference and the limited use of voice mail in Germany, you can see that the mere act of contacting the person you need can be a huge challenge. An American calling from New York needs to place the call by 10:00 AM to reach his German colleague at 4:00; a caller from L.A. has to rise early indeed to speak directly with someone in Germany.

Additional benefits vary by company. For example, your package might also include *Wohngeld* (housing subsidy), *Kindergeld* (child subsidy), subsidized travel to and from work, or subsidized (or free) lunch. All companies are also obliged to pay their employees a bonus equivalent to their monthly salaries, commonly called the thirteenth-month salary. This extra money comes at the end of each year.

Germany also has a wide social net, including *Arbeitslosengeld* (unemployment benefits) and *Arbeitslosenhilfe* (unemployment assistance), *Kurzarbeitergeld* (shortened work hours benefits) should your company have to shorten your work hours for a legitimate economic reason (preferable to layoffs), pensions (company pensions are also popular), and even industry-specific allowances.

If your company has a free cafeteria for employees, you may get your daily meal for nothing, but as the saying goes, there is no such thing as a free lunch. German salaries are heavily taxed—up to 53%—to help fund the cost of all of the benefits they receive. Because of the high tax rate, many employees would prefer to receive more benefits than a higher salary; in the final analysis, an attractive benefit package can be more valuable than your gross salary.

The German Social Insurance Law controls employer contributions to health, pension, unemployment, and assistance insurance programs. Both workers and employers contribute to the national health insurance program as well as to mandatory unemployment insurance.

THE GERMAN WORKFORCE

Germany boasts one of the most highly educated workforces in the world. It is also the best paid, although there is no legal minimum wage. All employment conditions and terminations are strictly regulated under German law. Unemployment is relatively low, due in part to government initiatives and laws designed to encourage full employment, such as short work weeks and subsidies that prevent layoffs in times of economic hardship.

Certification is required to perform most blue- and white-collar jobs. Germany ensures that young people receive appropriate preparation through a system that combines education and practical training. Skilled workers must spend a significant amount of time in apprenticeship or on-the-job training programs in order to receive certification. Continuing education is also important, and many people take advantage of seminars and professional skills courses whenever possible.

Following reunification, Germany experienced many labor-related problems. While East Germany boasted full employment, the reality was that there was a significant amount of hidden unemployment, underemployment, and redundancy. In addition, the quality of the education system and technology in the east was inferior to that in the west. All of this combined to create two generations of workers who were not as qualified as their western counterparts. As reunification brought new technology and new ideas to the east, workers in unproductive and obsolete jobs were laid off faster than new jobs were created. The government sought to balance this with vocational retraining, early retirement, job creation, and other programs. The government also ensured that sufficient social security was available to those who remained unemployed. In the years following reunification, Germany has managed to stabilize unemployment, but the issue remains of great concern, and the government continues to implement measures to combat it.

UNIONS

The German workforce is highly unionized, with about 37% of employees belonging to a trade union. Germany has a number of labor organizations, the largest of which are the *Deutscher Gewirkschaftsbund* (DGB; German Trade Union Federation), the *Deutsche Angestellten-Gewerkschaft* (DAG; German Union of Salaried Employees), the *Deutscher Beamtenbund* (German Civil Servants' Union), and the *Christlicher Gewerkschaftsbund Deutschlands* (CGD; Christian Trade Union Federation of Germany). Each of these is a federation of affiliated trade unions.

The DGB is by far the largest labor organization, with almost 10 million members in its 16 member unions. The DGB is organized along industry lines, not by job. The bookkeeper, the engineer, and the janitor at Siemens all belong to the same union.

Closed shops, where management can hire only union members, do not exist in Germany. Every employee has the right to choose whether or not to join a union.

Employers, too, have representation in the form of industry-based associations. The central organization for employer associations is the *Bundesvereinigung der Deutschen Arbeitgeberverbände* (BDA; Confederation of German Employers' Associations).

Employees and employers are considered partners in business. When their interests clash, collective agreements are negotiated by their representatives. Wages, holidays, benefits, pension and retirement ages, and general working conditions are all the concerns of labor organizations.

Unions, while politically independent, can nevertheless be powerful political movers. They frequently comment on the political issues of the day and actively seek to influence ones that concern their goals.

Over the years, unions have successfully:

- reduced working hours
- increased wages and salaries
- lengthened holidays and increased holiday pay
- provided more than 80% of workers an additional holiday allowance.

They continue to push for vocational assistance and equal input in management decisions (a measure stringently resisted by management). Despite not having equal power in management matters, the unions are able to ensure that major employee concerns such as expansion, layoffs, plant closings, and so on are given as much attention as capital issues.

The workers' right to strike is balanced by the employer's right to lock them out. There are few strikes in Germany, proof that both employees and employers are willing to negotiate their differences.

OFFICE SPACE

If an initial glance at the inside of a German company convinces you that German and American office spaces are the same, look again. It is true that German offices contain both office space and cubicles. Interoffice status is measured in similar ways: having an office, the size and location of the office, etc. However, there are some differences that you need to be aware of before you sit down with your German colleagues.

If you enter a German's office and sit down, you may be tempted to pull your chair closer to your colleague's desk. Resist the temptation, though. Germans have a larger comfort zone of personal space than Americans. They tend to stand about a meter apart when conversing, and this distance is also reflected in the placement of furniture. So you may find yourself feeling as if you are pitching your product from across the room. Don't take this personally, because it is not meant that way. And, more importantly, do not rearrange the furniture, which will encroach on your German colleague's personal space and can be highly insulting as well.

Germans can be quite territorial and will often clearly mark their personal space through the placement of furniture. Privacy is also very important. Doors, both at home and at the office, are kept closed. This does not by any means signify that a manager, for example, is uninterested in his subordinates. Rather it indicates a level of trust in their ability to perform.

A closed door also does not mean that someone is unavailable. Simply knock and wait to be asked to enter. In some offices with a more informal environment, co-workers knock and then enter without waiting for a response. You should not under any circumstance simply burst in on someone without warning.

WOMEN IN BUSINESS

Women and men have equal rights under the German *Grundgesetz*, or Constitution. Despite their legal claim to equality, few women in Germany today, 50 years after the ratification of the Constitution, would agree that they stand on equal ground with men.

Although the status of women in society has improved over the years, the traditional beliefs of a woman's "place" die hard. While in theory the traditional *Kinder, Kirche, Küche* (children, church, kitchen) are no longer considered the only appropriate interests of women, there are still challenges for the modern German woman.

What have women accomplished in the last five decades? Legislative changes have given women equal rights in the matters of marriage and divorce (especially when it comes to property owner-ship). The Act on the Equal Treatment of Men and Women at Work, enacted in 1980, prohibits employment discrimination on the basis of sex. Other statutory measures have allowed women more access to positions in federal and public agencies and have been aimed at eliminating sexual harassment in the workplace. Regulations have been put into place to prevent women from losing their positions if they become pregnant. And the education system has offered girls and women more opportunities for advanced education and train-ing. In recent years, women have been appointed or elected to high-level positions such as *Bundestag* president, Defense Commissioner, and state Minister-President.

Despite these advances and the vision of various pieces of legis-lation, women have not yet achieved full equality, especially in the business environment. Some of the remaining challenges are:

- Women typically receive lower wages than men. Although a woman can go to court in cases where she is receiving less pay for equal work, there remains a large gap between what is considered "woman's work" and what is "man's work." Jobs most often held by women receive the lowest wages.
- Although women are eligible to attend any vocational training program they desire, they are not offered as many apprentice-ships (necessary for certification) as their male counterparts.
- In economic downturns, women lose their jobs at a significantly higher rate than men.
- The structure of society remains such that women are charged with the majority of family-related chores, such as cooking, shopping, etc. The infrastructure has not developed in such a way as to accommodate the needs of women who work as well as maintain family responsibilities. Restricted shopping hours, the difficulty of finding child care, and school schedules that do not complement business hours all combine to make it difficult for women to juggle family and career.

Leading business positions continue to be filled by men. Although women make up over 50% of the labor force, 82% of executive positions are held by men. In general, the number of women in business and professions is lower than in the United States. Many professions, such as architecture and engineering, remain bastions of male dominance while women are relegated to secretarial positions. Women who wish to enter a traditionally male profession face the same hurdle as women around the world: people are inclined to hire other people like them. When a man is doing the hiring, it's difficult for a woman to break into male-dominated areas. The situation in Germany, as elsewhere, is slowly changing as more and more women become qualified in all areas of expertise and little by little begin to create a presence in leadership and management positions.

Tips for Women in Business

Once in a management position, most women face the additional challenge of establishing credibility and continually proving ability. More than one woman has reached a leadership position only to find that she was under constant scrutiny or was not being taken seriously.

American women who find themselves in positions of authority in Germany sometimes feel an added burden to prove themselves. In addition, some of the general protocol is different from what they are used to, as the traditional courtesy extended to women by men does have a place even in the modern German workplace. Following are some tips to position yourself favorably in Germany.

- Clearly define your role from the moment you arrive on the scene. Be sure your colleagues are aware of your authority. Don't abuse it, but don't shirk it either.
- Establish your credentials and ability to do your job in a forthright, but not overbearing, manner. Being introduced to your colleagues by a respected individual, such as a superior, can help establish credibility.

- Refrain from any behavior or gestures that could possibly be construed as flirtatious or as a "come-on."
- Don't dress in such a way as to suggest you are trying to use your sexuality, not your intelligence, to accomplish your goals.
- Business dress is generally more conservative in Germany than in the United States. Try to match the dress of your male counterparts. Modestly cut clothes are recommended for a professional look; avoid short skirts, low-cut blouses, and gaudy jewelry.
- Once you have spent some time in your work environment, you can decide if a less conservative look is acceptable and add brighter colors, etc., as appropriate.
- German men generally treat women with a great deal of courtesy, even in the workplace.
- A man may wait for a woman to initiate a handshake.
- The true Continental greeting from a man is a kiss on the hand (more of a kiss above your hand; there is usually no actual contact). Although this happens infrequently (it is a more likely response from an older man), if you find your hand being raised for a kiss, don't pull away and don't show embarrassment.
- Men will probably open doors for you, light your cigarette, hold your chair, help you with your coat, etc. Don't be offended by it; accept graciously.
- On the street a man walks closest to the curb; otherwise he walks on the woman's left. A man will walk between two women; a woman will walk between two men. These customs have their roots in Germany's past. Men protected women from potential danger from the street—not to mention dirty water tossed from a window above. Standing on a lady's left allowed the gentleman to draw his sword if the need arose. Custom places the man in the best position to protect the woman. Note that these relative positions are not consciously assumed; they simply happen. A German man might feel vaguely uncomfortable if he is

improperly placed in relation to a female companion, without really knowing why.

- Men will almost always stand when meeting a woman for the first time or when a woman enters the room, and will remain standing until she takes a seat. Only much older or high-ranking men are potentially exempt from this courtesy. Women do not generally rise for other women.

BUSINESS STEP-BY-STEP

Now that we've taken a look at the overall structure and atmosphere of business in Germany, let's take a look at the specifics of doing business in Germany.

Germans have a reputation of being quite formal when it comes to business. While this is generally true, there are many factors that can influence the level of formality of any given situation. Certain industries, such as advertising or entertainment, are less formal than others. Younger employees are usually less formal than the previous generation, newer companies less formal than old, established companies. When you add the nature of the interaction—a conversation between two colleagues or an important negotiation—it becomes clear that one can at best attempt to define only the general characteristics of German business. That information can be helpful, however, in evaluating each situation on a case-by-case basis. The golden rule for the foreigner in Germany is to begin by being formal. By doing so you are showing respect, not taking liberties that aren't necessarily granted, and avoiding offense. Your German colleagues will let you know if and when a more relaxed atmosphere is appropriate.

APPOINTMENTS

Appointments are necessary; punctuality at appointments is essential. Make appointments well in advance and notify the other person if you must cancel. Preferred times for business appointments are between 11:00 AM and 1:00 PM or between 3:00 and 5:00 PM. Late-afternoon appointments are common. It is advisable not to try to schedule appointments or meetings on Friday afternoons without

first checking, since many offices close early due to the typical 35- to 37-hour work week.

When you arrive at an appointment, remember that handshakes are the accepted greeting in business situations. Greet everyone with a handshake upon entering and again when leaving. A short, firm handshake is usually appropriate, but don't squeeze someone's hand either. A handshake that is too soft indicates insecurity or indifference to a German.

Using last names is common in business; don't assume that you will be on a first-name basis with anyone, even your colleagues. Even if you are on familiar terms with a co-worker, you will probably need to revert to last names at certain times, such as in a meeting or when referring to your colleague to the boss. In more modern companies, it is common to use first names, but still use the formal form of "you" (*Sie*).

BUSINESS CARDS

The business card is quite important in Germany, more so than in the United States. Keep several business cards with you at all times.

German business cards are very detailed. They include the usual information: name and business title, address, e-mail address, and telephone and fax numbers. However, they also include any degrees you hold, your professional title (i.e., Dr. Hans-Jürgen Müller), and sometimes even the year that the company was founded.

If you will be living in Germany, or if you do business there frequently, it is advisable to have your business card translated into German on one side. The information on your business card is not just contact information. It lets your German colleagues know what level of responsibility you have within the company. Therefore an accurate translation of your job title into German is essential. Take care not to translate literally, as some positions have similar-sounding titles but cannot necessarily be equated in terms of responsibilities. Determine what title actually describes the level of responsibility you hold in the company.

Present your card when you first meet someone. It's not necessary to press additional cards on your business contacts each time you see them. Hand out your cards selectively; don't just dole them out like playing cards. Business cards should be treated respectfully. Be sure you hand the card to the person; don't just toss it on the person's desk. Don't just stick someone's card in your back pocket, even if it is in your wallet, where it will be sat on, and don't use it as scrap paper. If you find it necessary to make a note on someone's business card, wait until you are out of his or her presence; this is not a common practice in Germany and some people take offense at it.

DRESSING FOR SUCCESS

German clothes tend to favor practicality. This does not mean that clothes are not stylish. On the contrary, Germans can be very stylish dressers. Most, however, prefer high-quality clothing that reflects a classic, timeless style over trendy fashions. Germans tend to dress more conservatively than Americans. You are unlikely to see scantily clad Germans unless you are at the beach.

Professional dress is a must in the average business environment. For men this means a suit and tie, for women a suit, dress, or equivalent business attire. Men do not often take off their jackets. If they have removed it in the privacy of their own office, they will put it on again before receiving a guest, going to a meeting, etc. You will probably see men's suits and shirts in a wider range of colors than in the United States. Dark suits are always appropriate, but for everyday wear the palette is much broader. For women in a German business environment it is advisable to keep skirts at a relatively modest length; very short skirts are inappropriate.

"Business casual" has not caught on in Germany. Seminars, conferences, and trade shows are not occasions to dress down. Improper dress may be construed as disrespect or lack of professionalism. The German businessman who attends a trade show, for example, is looking for someone who is serious about doing business; casual dress means a casual attitude toward business.

Germans in general don't care to look like slobs in public. Shorts and sweatpants aren't common except when participating in sports or exercise. Even when going out to the store, a German woman will probably wear a simple dress or clean, presentable (wrinkle- and hole-free) clothes. It's not common to see women wearing shorts and a bikini top or Spandex biking shorts, or a shirtless man mowing the lawn.

But don't get the idea that Germans are prudish. Mixed saunas and nude sunbathing are commonplace. Nude bathing areas are marked FKK (for *Freikörperkultur*) or form spontaneously in certain beach areas or remote lakes. You may also see topless women at the public swimming pool.

OFFICE RELATIONSHIPS

Office relationships in Germany reflect German culture. Trust between co-workers is essential; friendship is not. The German office environment in general is more formal and "businesslike" than the typical American one. The day begins with a greeting of *Guten Tag* to each person you encounter, often accompanied by a handshake. Most colleagues address each other with the more formal *Sie* (you) rather than *du*, the informal form. Colleagues who work together for years refer to each other as Herr Kunert and Frau Bernhard, not Richard and Silke. While things have become somewhat more informal in some German offices over the years, especially in younger businesses and among younger workers, it would be a mistake to assume that you can be as informal in a German office as you can in an American office.

German formality extends to other aspects of office protocol. Germans are not likely to "drop by" someone's desk to chat or even to discuss business. Instead, it is more common to agree with a colleague on a specific time to get together to discuss the matter.

Americans who work with Germans often get the feeling that the atmosphere in Germany is cold and indifferent. The truth, though, is that the greater respect for personal privacy and more formality create a more businesslike environment in which the Germans are quite comfortable. Interoffice relationships are amiable without being overly intrusive.

In an American office, much of the communication occurs via informal channels. Information is exchanged at the coffeemaker or water cooler or in the hallways as often as it is by more formal channels—and often more quickly as word wends its way through the office grapevine. What serves as both an exchange of information and the nurturing of friendly office relationships in an American office is largely viewed by the German eye as a waste of time. This is a crucial difference between the German and American work environments: Germans prefer efficiency, while Americans value a friendly atmosphere. While the Americans are questioning the dedication of the German employee who leaves at 5:00 every day, the Germans are wondering how on earth the Americans ever accomplish anything, since they always seem to be chatting rather than working. Put together, Americans are often disappointed at the "cold" German environment, with its lack of camaraderie, whereas the Germans are frustrated at the lack of efficiency on the part of the Americans.

Germans, especially white-collar workers, are quite conscious of their status and rank within the company, and they find it very insulting to be given an order by someone who is their equal, or to be talked down to. This is especially important when interacting with your German colleagues' secretaries or other support staff—or your own. Secretaries, regardless of age, should be addressed by their last names, never by first name or, even worse, by an endearment (akin to "Hon" or "Sweetie" in English). In general, you should treat them as the professionals they are. Remember that in Germany secretaries are part of yet another profession that requires extensive training and certification.

GIFT GIVING

Business gift giving is very restrained. Gifts are not exchanged at meetings, but small gifts may be given at the end of a successful negotiation. Books, music, liquor, or gifts from your home country are appropriate. Items with a prominently displayed company logo are in poor taste. Co-workers generally do not exchange gifts. Many companies do not have a Christmas party; interoffice gift exchanges, such as the "secret Santa," are not known in Germany.

Avoid giving gifts that are too personal (i.e., perfume or jewelry) or too extravagant, especially in business. Personal gifts are confined to immediate family and intimate relationships. Knives and other pointed objects are considered unlucky by the more superstitious.

MEETINGS

Punctuality is ever a virtue in Germany. It is especially important to be on time to business meetings and appointments. Meetings generally take place behind closed doors, and are generally more formal than the typical American meeting, in terms of both conduct and protocol. For example, if you have removed your suit jacket in the privacy of your office, you will want to put it back on before going to the meeting or receiving someone in your office.

If the meeting includes representatives from another company, beverages are likely to be served. However, there will be little, if any, chit-chat before the meeting commences. It's quite usual to walk into an office and begin the business discussion immediately after introducing yourself and exchanging business cards.

Be prepared for any meeting you attend. Germans are on the whole very detail-oriented. Most are specialists, not generalists. If you show up uninformed, or underinformed, you will at best place yourself in a negative light. At worst, you could jeopardize the deal. Remember, Germans place a high value on real know-how and expect individuals to know their stuff backwards and forwards, inside and out. Especially for important meetings, it's wise to spend some prep time anticipating all possible questions and preparing responses. If you place yourself in the position of continually saying "I'll get back to you with that information," your colleagues will eventually lose confidence in your ability to do your job.

Many Germans take long vacations (often a four-week block) during the months of July, August and December. Vacations are generally scheduled several months or more before the event, so you should be able to check well in advance so you will be able to work around your German colleagues' vacation plans. "Vacation" is more often called a "holiday" by Germans, most of whom have learned British English. Don't confuse a vacation "holiday" with one of Germany's many legal holidays. Don't expect a German to give up or postpone his or her vacation for business reasons.

NEGOTIATING AND PERSUADING

Negotiating in Germany, as in the United States, is for the purpose of finalizing an agreement. When you put together your negotiating team, it is important to include the proper technical experts as well as the folks responsible for the business side of things. Germans expect technical information and are impressed by a precise, concrete, and systematic presentation of facts.

The more important the negotiation, the more high-level executives will be involved. It is often not necessary for the very top level of management to be involved in negotiations. They are more often handled by representatives of the appropriate departments.

If the negotiation is in its beginning stages, it is unlikely that the German team will be able to commit without approval from above. As the negotiation proceeds, the appropriate people will be updated and an offer can be made.

German negotiations can take a considerable amount of time. The signing of the contract is serious business. A written contract is an absolute guarantee. Before that point can be reached, all issues will have been discussed thoroughly and all details worked out. Americans meeting with Germans often find themselves unprepared for the depth of detail required by the German team.

Once the ink is dry on the contract, a celebration may be called for, again depending on the magnitude of the deal. A few days of negotiation might call for a drink or dinner for the participants. An important deal, such as a joint-venture agreement, calls for a more elaborate event attended by the company's chief executives, perhaps a champagne dinner. As is the case for the vast majority of business entertaining, post-negotiation festivities, big or small, take place in a restaurant rather than in someone's home.

Tips for Business Entertaining

- Business entertaining is usually done in restaurants, not in homes.
- Business lunches are much more common than business breakfasts.
- Lunch with a business colleague is usually more social than business. Don't try to steer the conversation immediately to business.
- Many Germans have a beer with their lunch. You should not, of course, return to the office staggering.
- A business dinner is a social event, complete with drinking and social conversation, not business discussions.
- Spouses are generally not included in business dinners. However, if your spouse is traveling with you, it is okay to inquire if he or she may join.
- Older people will more often socialize with people of the same social level. The younger generation is generally more open.
- Americans can expect that their German business partner will be very hospitable to them.
- Be on time for all events, business or social.
- A thank-you note or a phone call following a social event is appropriate and appreciated.

SPEECHES AND PRESENTATIONS

Not all of the tips that you got from your book on successful presentations will work in Germany. One typical American technique for setting the tone of a presentation or speech is to begin with a joke.

This often falls flat in Germany. For one thing, a presentation in a business environment is business, not entertainment. And for another, humor does not travel well. Even if your audience understands the words, the content may be lost. That's not to say that the Germans are humorless—they aren't. It's just not likely that a joke that has them rolling in the aisles at home will have the same impact in Germany. This also does not mean that your presentation or speech should be staid and boring. Your goal is to keep your presentation interesting, yet professional.

Obviously the content of your presentation should be tailored to your audience. However, it's important to keep in mind that Germans are likely to require a depth of information that an American audience would not. Therefore you must be thoroughly prepared for your presentation, and be prepared for the questions that will follow. A presenter who is not exceptionally well informed about the topic he or she is discussing will lose credibility. This includes being able to answer any questions that crop up.

The best presentation style for a German audience is a logical presentation of information laid out in a clear, concise format. If you intend to show only the resulting information, be prepared to back up your conclusions with the applicable research data, financial models, etc. Most Germans expect to be shown background information and the process that led to your conclusions.

BUSINESS COMMUNICATION

Business communication in Germany relies heavily on the telephone and fax machine. Internet communication hasn't yet made the inroads it has in the United States.

If you are trying to make an initial contact with a German company, such as locating a supplier or a buyer for your product, a personal introduction can be very beneficial, even though it is not absolutely necessary. A personal contact can be made in a variety of ways, at trade shows or through mutual business contacts. However, in the event that an introduction is not possible, it is quite acceptable to use the telephone to make contact with a representative of the company.

Once you are doing business in Germany, your day-to-day communications will continue to be via telephone and fax. While most people in the office have e-mail, it is not the prevailing means of communication. Although you may check your e-mail hourly, don't assume that your German counterparts do. Other forms of communication technology, such as video conferencing, are infrequently used.

Telephone communication can be frustrating at times, since not all companies have voice mail. An added complication is that people do not customarily answer other people's phones, so you may not be able to leave a message. The only solution is to continue to call until the person returns to his or her desk.

There is also more interoffice use of the telephone. As mentioned earlier, a German is less inclined to stop by someone's office or desk. It is much more common to call that person on the telephone.

DECISION-MAKING

The typical structure of authority in a German company is vertical. Decisions are made by a few people at the top of the organization and filter down to the lower levels. There is, however, a measure of consensus-building in that all of the appropriate people must be consulted before the decision can be finalized. For example, if a decision will affect several departments, the heads of those departments must all be informed and brought into the discussion of the merits of the decision. When you combine that with the fact that the Germans are apt to discuss the decision in considerable detail, the result, of course, is that decision-making can take a long time. Decisions are rarely, if ever, made on the spot. It is more characteristic for a German to prefer to spend as much time as necessary analyzing the issue rather than rushing into things. This is contrary to the American preference of taking action with the assumption that details can be refined or changes made later, if necessary. Time is never the first priority in German decision-making. And because of the attention to detail that goes into the process, the final decision is essentially immutable.

While major decisions are made at the top, German employees do have considerable empowerment for making decisions within the purview of their jobs.

The nature of the German hierarchy, combined with the compartmentalization of the typical German organization, makes it necessary to locate and deal directly with the person who is specifically responsible for the issue or area you need addressed.

MANAGING

The German manager is of a different breed from the American manager. Unlike the American manager who has a degree in business, the German manager is highly qualified in his field. The head of Deutsche Bank has a degree in finance, the head of Siemens a degree in engineering. Technical qualifications are more valued in a manager than "soft" skills.

A German manager expects a lot from his or her employees. Employees are expected to perform well with no coddling and without constant supervision. The manager in turn sets the standards and acts as a role model. In turn, German employees expect their managers to be highly competent in their field. Good managers work as hard as their subordinates and continually perform competently. And of course as leaders they must be concerned about the careers of their subordinates and provide them a challenging and rewarding work environment and opportunities for advancement.

EVALUATIONS, FEEDBACK, AND ADVANCEMENT

Because everyone in the office is expected to perform competently and efficiently, it is not common to hear words of encouragement in the normal course of events. No one gives or receives praise for simply doing the job. Americans entering the German environment often become confused about their performance because they are not receiving the positive feedback that they are accustomed to. Alternatively, Germans can lose respect for an American supervisor who seems to be complimenting their every move. To a German this can feel very patronizing and sends the signal that the manager is not confident that the employee can do his or her job adequately.

As a rule, employees are evaluated somewhat informally. Evaluations are done by the supervisor, rarely if ever by peers, and never by subordinates. Most companies have no formal system of routine evaluation in place. The old adage "No news is good news" applies in most situations. Since supervisors don't look over your shoulder when things are going well, you know there is a problem when you are being scrutinized.

Reward for exceptional work can take many forms. Money is a tried-and-true motivator in Germany. However, other incentives can also be quite successful. For example, because of the heavy taxation that applies to bonuses and other monetary rewards, an employee might prefer to receive a different type of benefit, such as an extra day off with pay. Praise and advancement are other ways good work is rewarded.

On the opposite side of the coin, substandard work must be dealt with. Part of the manager's job is to let people know what is expected of them and to provide guidance. No one likes to confront employees with a problem, but all managers encounter that type of situation from time to time. Negative feedback is best given in private. If you are meeting with someone to for this purpose, it is important to keep emotions out of the picture. Don't flare up or raise your voice.

Because firing an employee is so difficult, it is necessary to follow the correct procedures leading up to dismissal. All meetings and discussions must be properly documented and the employee must be informed at all stages of the proceedings. We'll get back to this in just a moment.

Advancement in Germany is based on ability, with a large dose of seniority thrown in. In most cases, one can expect to move up the corporate ladder at a steady but sedate pace, assuming you have the proper qualifications for a job. Promotion can be limited by the size or structure of the company. Because of the importance of area-specific expertise and the amount of compartmentalization in most German companies, lateral promotions are not common. Therefore, one is largely limited to the opportunities that exist in one's department or division.

HIRING AND FIRING

The process of hiring and firing employees in Germany is quite complex. Because Germany has stringent laws regarding the firing of employees, the best solution is to hire the right people at the beginning.

When hiring a new employee, the most important qualification is technical ability. A secretary must be able to type, an engineer must be able to build a bridge. Hiring is job-specific. The type of management-track programs that many American companies have adopted and filled with recent MBA grads is not common in Germany. America is the land of opportunity for the generalist; Germany is the paradise of the specialist.

Certification in your area of expertise is crucial. This applies whether you are a carpenter, a secretary, or an architect. Germany's education program provides numerous technical apprenticeships and other training programs to prepare young people for entry into the work world. Many Americans are surprised to find that their secretary received extensive training and that their roofer is actually a master craftsman.

Once a person has been hired, it is very difficult to fire that person without sufficient cause. A *fristlose Kündigung* (instant dismissal) can be given only for reasons such as theft, violence, or industrial espionage. Any other type of infraction or underperformance that may lead to dismissal will need very careful and detailed documentation. The employer must consult the *Betriebsrat* (Workers' Council) prior to the dismissal. The *Betriebsrat* can in turn lodge a protest against the dismissal. If this happens, the employer must retain the employee until the matter is resolved by the *Arbeitsgericht* (Labor Court). Any time an employee is dismissed, he or she has the right to appeal the matter to the *Arbeitsgericht*. The employer must present adequate evidence to support the dismissal; if the court rules in favor of the employee, he or she must be reinstated or a settlement for wrongful dismissal must be paid.

Layoffs are equally difficult. The company must prove that the layoffs are an economic necessity. In matters such as this the *Betriebsrat* must be involved. It will often seek to find an alternate solution, or, if the layoff is inevitable, to find a way to mitigate economic hardship for the employees to be laid off. Even if the layoff is accepted by the employees, the employer must follow certain guidelines relating to the amount of notice given the employees and layoff benefit packages.

To counterbalance the strict employment laws, most companies have a *Probezeit* (trial period) in effect for new hires. This time, usually from three to six months, allows the company and the employee to decide if the fit is right for both. The employee can be terminated at any point during the trial period without repercussion.

A NOTE ON USING INTERPRETERS

Since many Germans, especially those involved in international business, speak English very well, interpreters are often not necessary. However, if you do find yourself in a situation that requires an interpreter, there are several things that you can do to make the experience run smoothly.

- Whenever possible, use an interpreter who is familiar with your industry and even with your company. If your company does not have access to a suitable individual and must hire someone unfamiliar to you or your company, arrange to meet with the interpreter before the meeting in order to brief him on your company, your goals, and your expectations. Provide the interpreter with as much documentation as possible to allow him or her to prepare for the meeting.

- If you happen to have a German-speaking team member and are relying on that person to interpret for the team, don't also expect him or her to enter into the negotiations. It not only becomes confusing, it is virtually impossible, because interpreting requires a great deal of focus and concentration. So even if a key member or members of your team speak German, it is still wise to have an official interpreter who is not part of the actual negotiation.

- If each team has an interpreter present, each will translate the comments of his or her respective team. If only one is present, he will obviously be responsible for all translation.

- Always address the person to whom the comment or question is directed, not the interpreter. This takes practice, as most people tend to automatically turn to face the interpreter.

- Don't overwhelm the interpreter with words. You should pause for interpretation after every two or three sentences.

- Try to keep your sentences as uncomplicated as possible. A long, rambling sentence is very difficult to translate.

- Keep your vocabulary as simple as the situation will allow. Hopefully you will have taken the time to ensure that the interpreter has a vocabulary compatible with your needs, and will have gone over any technical details with him or her.

- Avoid slang and colloquialisms. They may not be understood or, potentially even more disastrous, they may be misunderstood if they are interpreted literally.

- The interpreter is not a machine. Interpreting takes an enormous amount of mental energy and is very draining. Allow at least a brief rest period after every hour or so. This is another argument in favor of having separate interpreters.

- If you are having trouble making yourself understood—and this goes for direct communication as well as interpreter-assisted communication—do not under any circumstance repeat your question or comment in ever-increasing volume. The problem is comprehension, not hearing. Rephrase the statement until you reach understanding.

EIGHT

LAST NOTES

We hope that this book has given you some insight into Germany and has suggested some ways to prepare yourself for a successful, rewarding experience dealing with Germans. The practical tips contained in this book should help you feel more comfortable as your journey begins, and the information on the German culture will help you navigate as your journey continues. Finally, you'll find a language section that contains the most essential words and phrases; remember that even a little bit of German will make a world of difference.

In addition to the specific information covered in these seven chapters, don't forget these important guidelines for cross-cultural interaction anywhere around the globe:

- Learn about the culture you are visiting. The better you understand a country's culture, the more prepared you will be to tune your skills to its frequency.
- Keep your sense of humor. Things are guaranteed to go wrong now and again and you will make mistakes. Your best defense is your ability to find humor in the situation.
- And finally, respect other cultures. Just because it's not the way you do things doesn't mean it's wrong.

Viel Glück (und viel Spaß) in the exciting new environment that awaits you in Germany.

NINE

Language

GERMAN ALPHABET AND PRONUNCIATION

ALPHABET

Letter	Name	Letter	Name	Letter	Name
a	*ah*	j	*yot*	s	*ess*
b	*beh*	k	*kah*	t	*teh*
c	*tseh*	l	*ell*	u	*oo*
d	*deh*	m	*em*	v	*fauh*
e	*eh*	n	*en*	w	*veh*
f	*eff*	o	*oh*	x	*iks*
g	*geh*	p	*peh*	y	*üpsilon*
h	*hah*	q	*ku*	z	*tsett*
i	*ee*	r	*err*		

LANGUAGE

VOWELS

long a	as in ah: "father"	Vater
short a	as in a: "cut"	Ratte
long ä	as in "hair"	spät
short ä	as in "men"	Männer
long e	as in "dare"	gehen
short e	as in "bent"	Adresse
e	at end of a word as in "pocket"	heute
long i, ie	as in "meet"	Liebe
short i	as in "ship"	Mitte
long o	as in "hope"	Bohne
short o	as in "tall", but shorter	kommen
long ö	similar to e in geben but with rounded lips	König
short ö	similar to short u but with rounded lips	können
long u	as in "mood"	Buch
short u	as in "bush"	dumm
long ü	as long i with rounded lips	früh
short ü	as short i but with rounded lips	Brücke
y	pronounced as long u	Typ

DIPHTHONGS

ai	as in "by"	Kai
ei	same as ai	Leine
au	as in "house"	Haus
äu	as in "boy"	häufig
eu	same as äu	Freund

CONSONANTS

b	as **b** in "bed"; at the end of a word as p in "trap"
c	as **k** in "keep"; rarely as ts in "cats"
d	as **d** in "date"; at the end of a word as t in "but"

f	as *f* in "fly"
g	as *g* in "garden"
h	as *h* in "hundred" sometimes not pronounced at all: **Schuh** ("shoe")
j	as *y* in "York"
k	as *c* in "cut"
l	as *l* in "life"
m	as *m* in "man"
n	as *n* in "never"
p	as *p* in "painter"
q	as *q* in "quality"
r	a little more rolled than in English
s	at the beginning of a word as *z* in "zoo"; at the end of a word or syllable as *s* in "son"
t	as *t* in "tea"
v	as *f* in "fair"
w	as *v* in "vain"
x	as *x* in "mix"
z	like the English combination **ts**

SPECIAL LETTER COMBINATIONS

ch	before the vowel sounds "eh," "ee," a sound near the English **h** in "hue": Kirche ("church") before all other vowel and consonant sounds, a guttural sound not existing in English but close to the **ch** in Scottish "loch": machen (to do) in certain words of foreign origin, as **K** in "Keep": Charakter ("character")
ck	as k: Scheck ("check")
ig	mostly as in "league," in northern Germany as **h** in "hue": billig ("inexpensive")
sch	as **sh**: Schuh ("shoe")
sp	at beginning of word or accented syllable, as shp: Spanien ("Spain")
st	at beginning of word or accented syllable, as sht: stehen ("to stand")

ng	as **ng** in "sing"
tz	similar to the English **ts**: Blitz ("lightning")
ß	called "es-tset"; used in place of "ss" in certain words, and pronounced "s": Paß ("passport")

THE GERMAN LANGUAGE

Word Order

Word order in a simple German sentence is the same as in English, subject–verb–object: *Ich sehe den Mann.* (I see the man.) However, the main verb must remain in the second position. If a word other than the subject precedes the verb, this reverses the order of the subject and the verb: *Jetzt sehe ich den Mann.* (Now I see the man.) Unlike verbs in English, German verbs or verbal elements are in certain circumstances found at the end of the sentence: *Ich sage, daß ich den Mann sehe.* (I'm saying that I see the man.) *Ich habe den Mann gestern gesehen.* (I saw the man yesterday.)

Articles and Nouns

All German nouns are capitalized and are one of three genders: masculine, feminine, or neuter. The definite articles *der* (m.), *die* (f.), and *das* (n.), and the indefinite articles *ein* (m. and n.) and *eine* (f.) change to indicate the case of the noun, that is, the function the noun serves grammatically. *Der Mann ist in der Küche.* (The man is in the kitchen. *Der Mann* = nominative case, subject.) *Wir sehen den Mann.* (We see the man. *Den Mann* = accusative case, direct object.) *Die Frau spricht dem Mann.* (The woman speaks to the man. *Dem Mann* = dative case, indirect object.) *Der Hut des Mannes ist schwarz.* (The man's hat is black. *Des Mannes* = genitive case, possessive.) Gender and case also play very important roles in pronoun usage and adjective agreement.

def. /indefinite	Nominative	Genitive	Accusative	Dative
masc.	der/ein	des/eines	den/einen	dem/einem
fem.	die/eine	der/einer	die/eine	der/einer
neut.	das/ein	des/eines	das/ein	dem/einem
plural	die	der	die	den

Adjectives

The ending of an adjective agrees with the gender, number, and case of the noun and reflects whether the definite article (*der/die/das*) or indefinite article (*ein-*) is used with the noun. To avoid mistakes with adjective endings, remember that all genitives, all datives, all plurals, and the masculine accusative adjectives have an *-en* ending. If an adjective replaces the article (uncommon) it takes the ending of the article it replaces (*das gute Buch = gutes Buch*)

after def. / indefinite	Nominative	Genitive	Accusative	Dative
masc.	-e /-er	-en	-en	-en
fem.	-e	-en	-e	-en
neut.	-e/-es	-en	-e/-es	-en
plural	-en	-en	-en	-en

Verbs

The endings of German verbs change to agree with their subjects in number and person: *Ich komme.* (I come.) *Du kommst.* (You come.) *Wir kommen.* (We come.) German verb tenses are very similar to English verb tenses. Most perfect tenses are formed with the auxiliary verb *haben* (to have): *Ich sehe.* (I see.) *Ich habe gesehen.* (I have seen./I saw.) *Ich hatte gesehen.* (I had seen.) *Ich werde gesehen haben.* (I will have seen.) But unlike English, German sometimes forms perfect tenses with the German auxiliary verb *sein* (to be): *Ich fliege.* (I fly.) *Ich bin geflogen.* (I have flown./I flew.) etc. The auxiliary verb "to be" is mostly used with verbs of movement.

PHRASES

You don't need to master the entire German language to spend some time in Germany, but taking charge of a few key phrases in the language can aid you in just getting by. The following supplement will allow you to get a hotel room, get around town, order a drink at the end of the day, and get help in case of an emergency.

Listen to the phrase on the enclosed CD and repeat what you hear in the space provided.

COMMON GREETINGS

Hello/Good morning.	Hallo/Guten Morgen.
Good evening.	Guten Abend.
Good-bye.	Auf Wiedersehen.
Title for a married woman or an older unmarried woman	Frau
Title for a young and unmarried woman	Fräulein
Title for a man	Herr
How are you? (informal)	Wie geht's?
Fine, thanks. And you? (informal)	Gut, danke. Und dir?
How are you? (formal)	Wie geht es Ihnen?
Fine, thanks. And you? (formal)	Gut, danke. Und Ihnen?
What is your name?	Wie heißen Sie?
My name is...	Ich heiße/Mein Name ist ...
Nice to meet you.	Freut mich./Sehr erfreut. (more formal)
I'll see you later.	Bis später.

POLITE EXPRESSIONS

Please.	Bitte.
Thank you.	Danke schön.

Thank you very much.	Vielen Dank.
You're welcome.	Bitte schön.
Yes, thank you.	Ja, danke.
No, thank you.	Nein, danke.
I beg your pardon.	Ich bitte um Verzeihung.
I'm sorry.	Das tut mit leid.
Pardon me. (informal)	Entschuldige.
Pardon me. (formal)	Entschuldigen Sie.
That's okay.	Schon gut.
It doesn't matter.	Macht nichts.
Do you speak English?	Sprechen Sie englisch?
Yes.	Ja.
No.	Nein.
Maybe.	Vielleicht.
I can speak a little.	Ich spreche ein bißchen.
I understand a little.	Ich verstehe ein bißchen.
I don't understand.	Ich verstehe nicht.
I don't speak German very well.	Ich spreche nicht sehr gut deutsch.
Would you repeat that, please?	Würden Sie das bitte wiederholen?
I don't know.	Ich weiß nicht.
No problem.	Kein Problem.
It's my pleasure.	Mein Vergnügen.

NEEDS AND QUESTION WORDS

I'd like ...	Ich möchte.../Ich hätte gern...
I need ...	Ich brauche...
What would you like?	Was wünschen Sie?
Please bring me ...	Bringen Sie mir bitte...
I'm looking for ...	Ich suche nach...
I'm hungry.	Ich habe Hunger.
I'm thirsty.	Ich habe Durst.
It's important.	Es ist wichtig.
It's urgent.	Es ist dringend.

How?	Wie?
How much?	Wieviel?
How many?	Wie viele?
Which?	Welcher? (m)/Welche? (f)/ Welches? (n)
What?	Was?
What kind of . . . ?	Was für ein (-e)...?
Who?	Wer?
Where?	Wo?
When?	Wann?
What does this mean?	Was bedeutet dies?
What does that mean?	Was bedeutet das?
How do you say . . . in German?	Wie sagt man...auf deutsch?

AT THE AIRPORT

Where is . . .	Wo ist ...
customs?	der Zoll?
passport control?	die Paßkontrolle?
the information booth?	die Information?
the ticketing counter?	der Ticketschalter?
the baggage claim?	die Gepäckausgabe?
the taxi stand?	der Taxistand?
the car rental?	die Autovermietung?
the subway?	die U-Bahn?
the bus stop?	die Bushaltestelle?

Is there a bus service to the city?	Gibt es eine Busverbindung in die Stadt?
Where are . . .	Wo sind ...
the international departures?	die Flugsteige für den internationalen Abflug?
the international arrivals?	die Flugsteige für internationale Ankunft?
Where are you from?	Woher kommen Sie?
I am an American.	Ich bin Amerikaner (m)/ Amerikanerin (f).
I am Canadian.	Ich bin Kanadier (m)/ Kanadierin (f).

AT THE HOTEL, RESERVING A ROOM

I would like a room.

Ich hätte gern ein Zimmer.

for one person
for two people
for tonight
for two nights
for a week

für eine Person
für zwei Personen
für diese Nacht
für zwei Nächte
für eine Woche

Do you have a different room?

Haben Sie ein anderes Zimmer?

with a bath
with a shower
with a toilet
with air-conditioning

mit Bad
mit Dusche
mit Toilette
mit Klimaanlage

How much is it?

Wieviel kostet es?

I'd like to have my bill, please.

Ich hätte gern die Rechnung, bitte.

AT THE RESTAURANT

Where can we find a good restaurant?

Wo können wir ein gutes Restaurant finden?

We'd like a(n) ... restaurant.

Wir möchten gern in ...

casual

ein unformales Restaurant gehen.

elegant

ein elegantes Restaurant gehen.

fast-food
inexpensive

einen Schnellimbiß gehen.
ein preiswertes Restaurant gehen.

seafood
vegetarian

ein Fischrestaurant gehen.
ein vegetarisches Restaurant gehen.

Café

das Café

A table for two, please.

Einen Tisch für zwei, bitte.

Waiter, a menu, please.

Herr Ober, die Karte, bitte.

I'd like the wine list, please.

Ich hätte gern die Weinkarte, bitte.

Appetizers

Vorspeisen

Main course	Hauptgericht
Dessert	Nachspeise/Nachtisch
What would you like?	Was wünschen Sie?
What would you like to drink?	Was möchten Sie gern trinken?
Can you recommend a good wine?	Können Sie einen guten Wein empfehlen?
Wine, please.	Einen Wein, bitte.
Beer, please.	Ein Bier, bitte.
I didn't order this.	Das habe ich nicht bestellt.
That's all, thanks.	Das ist alles, danke schön.
I'd like the check, please.	Ich hätte gern die Rechnung, bitte.
Cheers! To your health!	Prost! Zum Wohl!

OUT ON THE TOWN

Where can I find ...	Wo finde ich ...
an art museum?	ein Kunstmuseum?
a museum of natural history?	ein Naturkundemuseum?
a history museum?	ein geschichtliches Museum?
a gallery?	eine Galerie?
interesting architecture?	interessante Architektur?
a church?	eine Kirche?
the zoo?	den Zoo?
I'd like ...	Ich möchte gern ...
to see a play.	ein Theaterstück sehen.
to see a movie.	einen Spielfilm sehen.
to go to a concert.	in ein Konzert gehen.
to go to the opera.	die Oper besuchen.
to go sightseeing.	eine Stadtrundfahrt machen.
to go on a bike ride.	eine Fahrradtour machen.

SHOPPING

Where is the best place to go shopping for ...	Wo kann man am besten ... kaufen?
clothes?	Kleidung

food?	Lebensmittel, -n
souvenirs?	Andenken
furniture?	Möbel
fabric?	Stoff
antiques?	Antiquitäten
books?	Bücher
sporting goods?	Sportartikel
electronics?	Elektronik
computers?	Computer

DIRECTIONS

Excuse me.	Entschuldigung.
Where is...	Wo ist . . .
the bus stop?	die Bushaltestelle?
the subway station?	die U-Bahnstation?
the rest room?	die Toilette?
the taxi stand?	der Taxistand?
the nearest bank?	die nächste Bank?
the . . . hotel?	das ... Hotel
To the right	(nach) rechts
To the left	(nach) links
Straight ahead	geradeaus
It's near here.	Es ist ganz in der Nähe.
Go back.	Gehen Sie zurück.
Next to	neben

NUMBERS

Cardinal

0	null	8	acht
1	eins	9	neun
2	zwei	10	zehn
3	drei	11	elf
4	vier	12	zwölf
5	fünf	13	dreizehn
6	sechs	14	vierzehn
7	sieben	15	fünfzehn

16	sechzehn	60	sechzig
17	siebzehn	70	siebzig
18	achtzehn	80	achtzig
19	neunzehn	90	neunzig
20	zwanzig	100	einhundert
21	einundzwanzig	1,000	eintausend
22	zweiundzwanzig	1,100	eintausendeinhundert
23	dreiundzwanzig	2,000	zweitausend
30	dreißig	10,000	zehntausend
40	vierzig	100,000	einhunderttausend
50	fünfzig	1,000,000	eine Million

Ordinal

first	(der/die/das) erste
second	(der/die/das) zweite
third	(der/die/das) dritte
fourth	(der/die/das) vierte
fifth	(der/die/das) fünfte
sixth	(der/die/das) sechste
seventh	(der/die/das) siebte
eighth	(der/die/das) achte
ninth	(der/die/das) neunte
tenth	(der/die/das) zehnte
eleventh	(der/die/das) elfte
twelfth	(der/die/das) zwölfte
thirteenth	(der/die/das) dreizehnte
fourteenth	(der/die/das) vierzehnte
fifteenth	(der/die/das) fünfzehnte
sixteenth	(der/die/das) sechszehnte
seventeenth	(der/die/das) siebzehnte
eighteenth	(der/die/das) achtzehnte
nineteenth	(der/die/das) neunzehnte
twentieth	(der/die/das) zwanzigste
twenty-first	(der/die/das) einundzwanzigste

twenty-second	(der/die/das) zweiundzwanzigste
thirtieth	(der/die/das) dreißigste
fortieth	(der/die/das) vierzigste
fiftieth	(der/die/das) fünfzigste
sixtieth	(der/die/das) sechzigste
seventieth	(der/die/das) siebzigste
eightieth	(der/die/das) achtzigste
ninetieth	(der/die/das) neunzigste
hundredth	(der/die/das) einhundertste
thousandth	(der/die/das) tausendste

TIME

What time is it?	Wieviel Uhr ist es?/Wie spät ist es?
It is noon.	Es ist Mittag.
It is midnight.	Es ist Mitternacht.
It is 9:00 AM.	Es ist neun Uhr.
It is 1:00 PM.	Es ist dreizehn Uhr.
It is 3 o'clock.	Es ist drei (fünfzehn) Uhr.
It is 5:15.	Es ist Viertel nach fünf./Es ist fünf (siebzehn) Uhr fünfzehn.
It is 7:30.	Es ist halb acht. /Es ist sieben (neunzehn) Uhr dreißig.
It is 9:45.	Es ist Viertel vor zehn./Es ist neun (einundzwanzig) Uhr fünfundvierzig.
Now	jetzt
Later	später
Immediately	sofort
Soon	bald

DAYS OF THE WEEK/MONTHS OF THE YEAR

Monday	Montag
Tuesday	Dienstag
Wednesday	Mittwoch

Thursday	Donnerstag
Friday	Freitag
Saturday	Samstag/Sonnabend*
Sunday	Sonntag

| **What day is today?** | Welcher Tag ist heute? |

January	Januar
February	Februar
March	März
April	April
May	Mai
June	Juni
July	Juli
August	August
September	September
October	Oktober
November	November
December	Dezember

What is the date today?	Welches Datum haben wir heute?
Today is Thursday, September 22nd.	Heute ist Donnertag der zweiundzwanzigste September.
Yesterday was Wednesday, September 21st.	Gestern war Mittwoch der einundzwanzigste September.
Tomorrow is Friday, September 23rd.	Morgen ist Freitag der dreiundzwanzigste September.

MODERN CONNECTIONS

Where can I find ...	Wo befindet sich ...
a telephone?	ein Telefon?
a fax machine?	eine Faxmaschine?
an Internet connection?	eine Internetverbindung?
How do I call the United States?	Wie rufe ich in die Vereinigten Staaten an?

*In northern Germany, *Sonnabend* is used, whereas *Samstag* is more popular in the south.

I need ...	Ich ...
a fax sent.	muß ein Fax schicken.
a hook-up to the Internet.	brauche einen Internetanschluß.
a computer.	brauche einen Computer.
a package sent overnight.	muß ein Packet mit Auslieferung am folgenden Tag schicken.
some copies made.	muß ein paar Kopien machen.
a VCR and monitor.	brauche einen Videorecorder und einen Monitor.
an overhead projector and markers.	brauche einen Overheadprojektor und Markierstifte.

EMERGENCIES AND SAFETY

Help!	Hilfe!
Fire!	Feuer!
I need a doctor.	Ich brauche einen Arzt.
Call an ambulance!	Rufen Sie einen Krankenwagen!
What happened?	Was ist passiert?
I am/My wife is/My husband is/ My friend is/Someone is ...	Ich bin/Meine Frau ist/Mein Mann ist/Mein(e) Freund(in) ist/Jemand ist ...
I am/Someone is very sick.	Ich bin/Jemand ist sehr krank.
I am/Someone is having a heart attack.	Ich habe/Jemand hat einen Herzinfarkt.
I am/Someone is choking.	Ich bekomme/Jemand bekommt keine Luft.
I am/Someone is losing consciousness.	Ich verliere/Jemand verliert das Bewußtsein.
I am/Someone is about to vomit.	Ich muß mich/Jemand muß sich übergeben.
I am/Someone is having a seizure.	Ich habe/Jemand hat einen Anfall.
I am/Someone is stuck.	Ich stecke/Jemand steckt fest.

I can't breathe.	Ich bekomme keinen Atem.
I tripped and fell.	Ich bin gestolpert und gefallen.
I cut myself.	Ich habe mich geschnitten.
I drank too much.	Ich habe zu viel getrunken.
I don't know.	Ich weiß (es) nicht.

I've injured my...	Ich habe ... verletzt.
head	mich am Kopf
neck	mir den Nacken
back	mir den Rücken
arm	mir den Arm
leg	mir das Bein
foot	mir den Fuß
eye(s)	mir das Auge/die Augen

I've been robbed.	Ich bin beraubt worden.

COMMON PROVERBS

Aller guten Dinge sind drei.
All good things come in threes.

Alter schützt vor Torheit nicht.
There's no fool like an old fool.
(lit.: Age doesn't protect one from foolishness.)

Aus den Augen, aus dem Sinn.
Out of sight, out of mind.

Blinder Eifer schadet nur.
Haste makes waste.
(lit.: Blind enthusiasm only causes damage.)

Das Bessere ist des Guten Feind.
Don't settle for second-best.
(lit.: The better is the enemy of the good.)

Dem Glücklichen schlägt keine Stunde.
A happy person is oblivious to time.
(lit.: The clock doesn't strike for the happy one.)

Der Apfel fällt nicht weit vom Stamm.
> Like father, like son.
> (lit.: The apple doesn't fall far from the tree.)

Der kluge Manr baut vor.
> The smart man thinks ahead.

Die Strafe folgt auf dem Fuße.
> Your sins will catch up with you.
> (lit.: Punishment is always right behind.)

Ein gutes Gewissen ist ein sanftes Ruhekissen.
> A clear conscience lets you sleep well.
> (lit.: A good conscience is a gentle pillow.)

Einem geschenkten Gaul schaut man nicht ins Maul.
> Don't look a gift horse in the mouth.

Es gibt nichts Gutes, außer man tut es.
> If you want something done right, do it yourself.
> (lit.: There's nothing good, other than what you do.)

Es ist nicht alles Gold was glänzt.
> All that glitters is not gold.

Es ist noch nicht aller Tage Abend.
> Don't count your chickens before they're hatched.
> (lit.: It's not the the end of time.)

Frisch gewagt ist halb gewonnen.
> Well begun is half done.
> (lit.: Bravely dared is half the battle.)

Geteilte Freud' ist doppelte Freud'.
> Shared joy is twice the joy.

Glaube kann Berge versetzen.
> Faith can move mountains.

Gut' Ding will Weile haben.
> Rome wasn't built in a day.
> (lit.: A good thing (work) takes time.)

Hochmut kommt vor dem Fall.
> Pride comes before a fall.

Humor ist, wenn man trotzdem lacht.
> Humor is laughing in spite of everything.

In der Not frißt der Teufel Fliegen.

>   Beggers can't be choosers.

>   (lit.: In desperation the devil eats flies.)

Keine Rosen ohne Dornen.

>   You have to take the bad with the good.

>   (lit.: No roses without thorns.)

Klappern gehört zum Handwerk.

>   You have to toot your own horn.

>   (lit.: Making noise is part of the trade.)

Lügen haben kurze Beine.

>   Lying won't get you anywhere.

>   (lit.: Lies have short legs.)

Man muss das Eisen schmieden, solange es noch heiß ist.

>   Strike while the iron is hot.

Man soll die Feste feiern, wie sie fallen.

>   Seize your opportunities.

>   (lit.: You have to celebrate the holidays as they come.)

Man soll nicht den Ast absägen, auf dem man sitzt.

>   Don't bite the hand that feeds you.

>   (lit.: Don't saw off the branch you're sitting on.)

Morgenstund' hat Gold im Mund.

>   The early bird catches the worm.

>   (lit.: Morning hours have gold in their mouths.)

Müßiggang ist aller Laster Anfang.

>   Idle hands are the devil's plaything.

>   (lit.: Idleness is the beginning of all vice.)

Nichts wird so heiß gegessen, wie's gekocht wird.

>   Nothing is as difficult as it seems at first.

>   (lit: Nothing is eaten as hot as it's cooked.)

Ohne Fleiß keinen Preis.

>   No pain, no gain.

>   (lit.: No reward without effort.)

Ordnung ist das halbe Leben.

>   Being organized is half of (a good) life.

Probieren geht über studieren.

>   Experience is the best teacher.

>   (lit.: Practice is better than theory.)

Reden ist Silber, schweigen ist Gold.

It's sometimes better not to say anything at all.

(lit.: Speaking is silver, being quiet is gold.)

Salz und Brot macht Wangen rot.

A good diet keeps you healthy.

(lit.: Salt and bread put color in your cheeks.)

Spieglein, Spieglein an der Wand.

Mirror, mirror on the wall. (Said if someone is overly vain)

Steter Tropfen höhlt den Stein.

Slow and steady wins the race.

(lit.: A continuous drip erodes the stone.)

Übermut tut selten gut.

Don't get over-enthusiastic.

(lit.: Extreme boldness rarely does any good.)

Übung macht den Meister.

Practice makes perfect.

(lit.: Practice makes the master.)

Vorsicht ist besser als Nachsicht.

Look before you leap.

(lit.: Foresight is better than hindsight.)

Was dem einen Recht ist, ist dem andern billig.

What's sauce for the goose is sauce for the gander.

(lit.: What is justice for one person is fair for the other.)

Was du nicht willst, das man dir tu', das füg' auch keinem andern zu.

Treat others as you want to be treated.

Was ich nicht weiß, macht mich nicht heiß.

What I don't know can't hurt me.

(lit.: What I don't know doesn't get me worked up.)

Was lange währt, wird endlich gut.

Patience pays off.

(lit.: What took a long time, will turn out well.)

Wenn die Katze nicht im Hause ist, tanzen die Mäuse auf dem Tisch.

When the cat's away, the mice will play.

Wenn zwei sich streiten, freut sich der dritte.

When two parties are fighting, the third is in a position to take advantage of the situation.

(lit.: When two are fighting, the third is the lucky one.)

Wer andern eine Grube gräbt, fällt selbst hinein.

> Whoever digs a hole (sets a trap) for others falls in
> it himself/herself.

Wer es nicht im Kopf hat muß es in den Beinen haben.

> If you don't use your head, you have to work twice as hard.
> (lit.: If you don't have it in your head, you have to have it in your
> legs. [Said to someone who often forgets])

Wer im Glashaus sitzt soll nicht mit Steinen werfen.

> People who live in glass houses shouldn't throw stones.

Wer nicht hören will, muß fühlen.

> Pay attention or suffer the consequences.
> (lit.: He who doesn't want to listen has to feel (the consequences).)

Wer nicht wagt, der nicht gewinnt.

> Nothing ventured, nothing gained.

Wer sich die Suppe eingebrockt hat, muss sie auch auslöffeln.

> You made your bed, now lie in it.
> (lit.: You made the soup, so eat it.)

Wer zuletzt lacht, lacht am besten.

> He who laughs last, laughs best.

Wie man in den Wald hereinruft, so schallt es heraus.

> You reap what you sow.
> (lit.: What you shout in the forest is what you hear in the echo.)

COMMON IDIOMATIC EXPRESSIONS

Alles in Butter!

> Everything is quite all right.
> (lit.: It's all [swimming] in butter.)

Bleiben Sie auf dem Teppich.

> Be realistic.
> (lit.: Stay on the carpet.)

Da sind Sie auf dem falschen Dampfer.

> There you are wrong.
> (lit.: On the wrong steamer)

Dann fresse ich einen Besen.
> I don't believe (in) it.
> (lit.: I'd eat a broom.)

Darauf können Sie Gift nehmen.
> You can bet on it.
> (lit.: You can take poison on that.)

Das ist das Ei des Kolumbus.
> That is exactly it!
> (lit.: That's Columbus's egg.)

Das ist doch kein Beinbruch.
> That's not a big problem.
> (lit.: No leg has been broken.)

Das ist ein Faß ohne Boden.
> It will never pay off.
> (lit.: That's a barrel without a bottom.)

Das ist ein heißes Eisen.
> We'd better leave that alone.
> (lit.: That's a hot iron.)

Das ist ein Sturm im Wasserglas.
> A lot of fuss over nothing.
> (lit.: That's a tempest in a water glass.)

Das ist ein Tropfen auf den heißen Stein.
> That's much too little.
> (lit.: A drop on a hot stone)

Das ist nicht mein Bier.
> That's not my responsibility.
> (lit.: That is not my beer.)

Die Würfel sind gefallen!
> A decision has been made.
> (lit.: The die has been cast.)

Ehe ich mich schlagen lasse?
> Before I let someone hit me?
> (Jokingly said, to finally give in to someone's offer)

Ehrenwort!
> Word of honor!

Ein Anblick für die Götter.

That is such a hilarious sight.

(lit.: A sight for the gods)

Eine Hand wäscht die andere.

You scratch my back, I'll scratch yours.

(lit.: One hand washes the other.)

Er/Sie findet immer ein Haar in der Suppe.

He/She always has to find something negative.

(lit.: Always finds a hair in the soup)

Er/Sie nimmt kein Blatt vor den Mund.

He/She speaks his/her mind.

(lit.: Doesn't take a leaf in front of his/her mouth)

Gehüpft wie gesprungen!

Six of one, half a dozen of the other.

(lit.: Hopped as jumped)

Geschmacksache, sagte der Affe und biß in die Seife.

To each his own.

(lit.: A matter of taste, said the monkey as he bit into the bar of soap.)

Hals und Beinbruch!

Break a leg!

(Wishing someone good luck before a performance.)

Halten Sie mich auf dem Laufenden.

Keep me posted.

Hand aufs Herz!

Be honest!

(lit.: Hand on your heart!)

Hinz und Kunz

Every Tom, Dick, and Harry.

Ich habe keine Ahnung.

I have no idea.

Ich verstehe nur Bahnhof!

I have no idea what you just said!

(lit.: All I understood is "train station.")

Irren ist menschlich.

To err is human.

Jetzt schlägt's aber dreizehn!
> That really does it!
> (lit.: Now the clock strikes thirteen.)

Können wir unter vier Augen sprechen?
> Can we talk in private?

Lassen Sie die Kirche im Dorf!
> Be realistic! (lit.: Leave the church in the village.)

Lassen Sie uns aus der Not eine Tugend machen.
> Make a virtue out of necessity.

Lassen Sie uns nicht den Amtsschimmel reiten.
> Let's not be overly bureaucratic; let's not get wrapped up in red tape.
> (lit.: Let's not ride the white horse of public office.)

Lieschen Müller
> The little guy (with no outstanding characteristics)

Machen Sie aus einer Mücke keinen Elefanten.
> Don't make a mountain out of a molehill.
> (lit.: Don't make an elephant out of a mosquito.)

Malen Sie nicht den Teufel an die Wand.
> Let's not focus on the worst.
> (lit.: Let's not paint the devil on the wall.)

Mein Name ist Hase!
> I don't have a clue!
> (lit.: My name is rabbit.)

Mir sind die Hände gebunden.
> My hands are tied.

Otto Normalverbraucher
> John Q. Public
> (lit.: Otto Normal-Consumer)

Sie haben den Nagel auf den Kopf getroffen.
> You hit the nail on the head.

Spaß beiseite!
> All joking aside.

Was verschafft mir die Ehre?
> Why am I being honored with your visit? (formal)

Welch Glanz in meiner Hütte.
> What an honor your visit is.
> (lit.: What a brightness in my hut.)

Wenn der Schuh paßt!

If the shoe fits!

Wenn man vom Teufel spricht.

Speak of the devil.

Wir können zwei Fliegen mit einer Klappe schlagen.

We can kill two birds with one stone.

Wir müssen am Ball bleiben.

We have to stay on the ball.

Wir wollen nicht den Bock zum Gärtner machen.

Let's not make a destructive decision.

(lit.: Let's not make a gardener out of the goat.)

Wollen Sie mich auf den Arm nehmen?

Are you pulling my leg?

BEFORE YOU GO

Passport. Be sure that each member of your family has one, and that each is valid for the length of your assignment. Children should have separate passports; otherwise they will not be allowed to travel alone or with an adult other than their parents, even in an emergency.

Visas. Check with the embassies of any countries you will be in for necessary visas. Requirements vary by country, especially for international relocation. As you travel, don't overlook the fact that some countries require a transit visa for people passing through the country, even if you don't get off your plane or train.

Vaccinations / inoculations. Check for recommended vaccinations or inoculations for the country you will be living in, as well as any countries you intend to visit. (This is listed on the U.S. Department of State Consular Information Sheet; see Travel Advisories below.) The Department of Health and Human Services' Office of Public Health Services is able to issue an International Certificate of Vaccination containing your personal history of vaccinations. The ICV is approved by the World Health Organization.

Insurance. Make sure that your insurance will cover you while you are abroad. Check now, before you need it. If it won't, do some research to find out how to supplement or change your insurance so that you are adequately covered.

International driver's permits. Although you can use your U.S. or Canadian driver's license in some countries, it is generally advisable to obtain an international driver's permit. This is available from the AAA for a small fee and does not require taking a test. International driver's permits are valid for one year; after that time, you may have to get a local driver's license. Be sure that you get a permit that is valid for the country(ies) you will be driving in.

Pets. Check with the consulate of your host country to find out about restrictions and requirements for bringing pets into the country. Most countries require a health and immunization certificate from a veterinarian; some have quarantine periods upon arrival.

Medical records. Obtain complete medical records for each member of your family. Have one copy on hand for the trip in case of an emergency.

Prescriptions and medication. If you or anyone in your family takes prescription medications, especially those containing narcotics, have your doctor give you a letter stating what the drug is and why it is necessary. Be sure you get a list of the Latin names of all prescription drugs from your doctor, since brand names vary from country to country. Take a six-month supply of any prescription medication, if possible. All medication, prescription or over-the-counter, should be in its original bottle and clearly labeled. Drug and narcotics laws are very strict in many countries, and you do not want to run afoul of them. Ask your dentist if it is advisable to have fluoride treatments, especially for children; most countries do not add fluoride to the water.

School records. If you have chosen a school for your child, you will probably have already made arrangements to forward your child's records. If not, be sure to request a complete set of records to take with you for each child. Don't forget school records, including diplomas and certificates, for yourself or your partner if either one of you might take continuing education classes while you're abroad!

Wills and guardianships. Your personal affairs should be in order before you leave. Your lawyer or a family member should have access to these documents in the case of an emergency.

Power of attorney. Assign power of attorney to act in your interest at home, if necessary. (A power of attorney does not have to be permanent and can be nullified when you return, if desired.)

Paying bills. If you have a mortgage or other payments that must be paid while you're abroad, decide how to handle them before you go. There are several options, including maintaining a checking account at home and paying bills yourself, arranging for your bank to pay them (not all banks offer this service), or having your lawyer, accountant, or a family member pay them.

Travel advisories. The U.S. Department of State publishes a 1- to 2-page consular information sheet on each country that covers basic topics such as medical and safety information, as well as addresses and phone numbers of U.S. consulates in the country. When necessary, travel advisories are released regarding areas of political instability, terrorist activity, etc. Check before you travel. (Consular information sheets and travel advisories are also available on many online services, such as CompuServe, and at the State Department Web site at www.state.gov)

Copies of important documents. Make two copies of important documents; take one with you and leave one with your lawyer or a family member. Important documents include:

- Passport (the inside front cover, which contains your passport number and other information)
- Visas, transit visas, and tourist cards
- Driver's license, international driving permit
- Insurance card and other information
- International Certificate of Vaccination, medical records

Special needs. If you or anyone in your family has any special needs, check that appropriate facilities and services are available from hotels and airlines. Not all are equipped to deal with infants, persons with physical disabilities, and other concerns such as medication that requires special handling or refrigeration.

Change of address. Be sure to inform all of the necessary people and companies of your change of address. Some companies will assess a service fee for mailing bills and statements internationally. Write to each company, and keep a copy of the notice in case a problem develops and to remind you what bills and statements you should be receiving. Don't forget the following:

- Banks where you are keeping local accounts or have loans
- Credit cards, including department store and gasoline cards
- Stockbroker or stock transfer agent, retirement account agents
- Lawyer
- Accountant
- Insurance company, including homeowner's, personal, medical, and life
- Tax offices in any city or state where you have property tax liabilities
- Voter registration office
- Magazines and periodicals
- Alumni association and professional memberships

Bank letter of reference. It is often difficult to establish banking services in a country where you have no credit history. It will help to have your bank or credit-card issuer write you a letter of good credit. Also helpful is a letter from your local office in your new country that states your salary. Some banks now have branches in many countries; you may be able to open an expatriate account at home before you go that will allow you access to bank services worldwide.

Close unnecessary accounts. However, you should leave open one or two key accounts that will retain your credit history for your return. Also make arrangements to terminate telephone, utility, garbage collection, newspaper delivery, and other services as necessary.

Inventory. An inventory of all of your belongings is helpful for shipping and insurance purposes. Enlist the help of an appraiser as necessary for items of value.

Packing. Put a card with your name and address inside each piece of luggage and each box being shipped. Don't put your passport in the boxes to be shipped!!

CONTACTS & RESOURCES

CHAMBER OF COMMERCE

In the United States:

New York
German American Chamber of Commerce
40 W 57th Street, 31st Floor
New York, NY 10029
Tel: (212) 974–8830
Fax: (212) 974–8867
Web site: www.gaccny.com
E-mail: info@gaccny.com

Chicago
German American Chamber of Commerce
401 North Michigan Ave., # 2525
Chicago, IL 60611–4212
Tel: (312) 644–2662

San Francisco

German American Chamber of Commerce
900 Front Street, # 300
San Francisco, CA 94111
Tel: (415) 983–9565
Fax: (415) 983–9560
E-mail: gaccsf@aol.com

In Germany:

Berlin
Fasanenstr. 85
10623 Berlin
Tel: (030) 315 10–0
Fax: (030) 315 10–278

Bonn
Adenauerallee 148
53113 Bonn
Postfach 1446, 53004 Bonn
Tel: (0228) 104–0
Fax: (0228) 104–15

Frankfurt
Börsenplatz 4
60313 Frankfurt
Tel: (069) 21 97–0
Fax: (069) 21 97–1424

Hamburg
Adolphsplatz 1
20457 Hamburg
Tel: (040) 36138–0
Fax: (040) 36138–401

Leipzig
Goerdelerring 5
04109 Leipzig
Tel: (0341) 1267–0
Fax (0341) 1267–421

München
Max-Joseph-Str. 2
80333 München
Tel: (089) 511–60
Fax: (089) 5116–306

Stuttgart
Jägerstr. 30
70174 Stuttgart
Tel: (0711) 20 05–0
Fax: (0711) 20 05–354

EMBASSIES/CONSULATES

German Embassy/Consulates in the United States:

German Embassy
4645 Reservoir Rd.
Washington, DC 20007–1998
Tel: (202) 298–4000
Fax: (202) 298–4249 or 333–2653

German Consulate General
871 United Nations Plaza
New York, NY 10017
Tel: (212) 610–9700
Fax: (212) 610–9702/3/4/5

German Consulate General
1960 Jackson Street
San Francisco, CA 94109
Tel: (415) 775–1061
Fax: (415) 775–0187
E-mail: gksf@pacbell.net

German Consulate General
1330 Post Oak Blvd., Suite 1850
Houston, TX 77056
Tel: (713) 627–7770
Fax: (713) 627–0506
E-mail: info@germanconsulatehouston.org

German Consulate General
6222 Wilshire Blvd., Suite 500
Los Angeles, CA 90048
Tel: (323) 930–2703
Fax: (323) 930–2805

German Consulate General
676 North Michigan Ave.
    (Entrance Huron Street),
    Suite 3200
Chicago, IL 60611
Tel: (312) 580–1199
Fax: (312) 580–0099

German Consulate General
100 N. Biscayne Blvd., Suite 2200
Miami, FL 33132–2381
Tel: (305) 358–0290
Fax: (305) 358–0307
E-mail: gc@german-consulate-miami.org *or*
    gk@gk-miami.de

German Consulate General
3 Copley Place, Suite 500
Boston, MA 02116
Tel: (617) 536–4414 or (617) 536–8172 (operator)
Fax: (617) 536–8573
E-mail: boston@germanconsulate.org

German Consulate General
Marquis Two Tower, Suite 901
285 Peachtree Center Ave., N.E.
Atlanta, GA 30303–1221
Tel: (404) 659–4760/61/62
Fax: (404) 659–1280

American Embassy/Consulates in Germany

Embassy of the United States in Berlin
Neustädtische Kirchstr. 4–5
10117 Berlin
Federal Republic of Germany
Tel: (030) 8305–0
Closed on American and German holidays

Consular Section:
Clayallee 170
14195 Berlin
Federal Republic of Germany

Non-Immigrant Visa Section:
Appointments through the Visa Hot line
For request from outside Germany:
Fax: 49 30 831– 4926
American Citizen Services:
Tel: (030) 832–9233
Fax: (030) 8305–1215

U.S. Consulate General Frankfurt
Siesmayerstr. 21
60323 Frankfurt
Federal Republic of Germany
Tel: (069) 7535–0
Fax: (069) 7535–2277

U.S. Consulate General Hamburg
Alsterufer 27/28
20354 Hamburg
Federal Republic of Germany
Tel: (040) 411 71–0
Fax: (040) 417–665

U.S. Consulate General Leipzig
Wilhelm-Seyfferth-Str. 4
04107 Leipzig
Federal Republic of Germany
Tel: (0341) 213–840

U.S. Consulate General Munich
Königinstr. 5
80539 München
Federal Republic of Germany
Tel: (089) 2888–0
Fax: (089) 280–9998

RESOURCES FOR MOVING ABROAD

German National Tourist Office
122 East 42nd Street, 52nd Floor
New York, NY 10168–0072
Tel.: (212) 661–7200
Fax: (212) 661–7174
Web site: www.visits-to-germany.com
E-mail: gntony@aol.com

Video Overseas, Inc.
246 8th Avenue, 2nd Floor
New York, NY 10011
Tel: (212) 645–0797 or (800) 317–6945
Fax: (212) 242–8144
Web site: www.videooverseas.com
*Household appliances and electronics that are adapted
or manufactured for international use.*

Air Animal, Inc. (U.S. and Canada)
Tel: (800) 635–3448
*Information and assistance on moving your
pet abroad.*

HELPFUL WEB SITES

Major search engines for German sites are Fireball, Altavista,
Hotbot, Lycos, and Excite. The top-level domain for Germany is .de
    Many large online services and portals have a mirror site in
Germany, i.e., MSN (Microsoft Network).

German Information Center The official site of the German consulate offers lots of facts on Germany and many links to other related sites: www.germany-info.org/

German Tourism Board This site offers travel arrangements and hotel guides, and a lot of useful information on exploring the most beautiful places in Germany: www.germany-tourism.de

Expatriates Working and Living in Germany expats.cjb.net; how to do everything right in Germany.

Escape Artist www.escapeartist.com; site on living, investing, and profiles in Germany.

Expat Exchange You can share opinions with other expatriates living in Germany, etc., at: www.expatexchange.com

Auf Wiedersehen Net Mainly targeted towards British living or moving to Germany, but a lot of info on this site is just as helpful to Americans or Canadians: www.guettier.btinternet.co.uk/expat/

www.fodors.com A site that has everything a traveler could possibly need, *fodors.com* lets you read up on hotels and restaurants, book reservations, and even create your own miniguide. There's also travel news, a bulletin board for sharing travel advice, tips on packing, and much more.

German Stock Exchange If you want to find out about the German stock exchange or other financial information in German, one of the many possibilities is: www.t-online.de/finanzen

German Telephone Directory An online telephone book including the Yellow Pages (*Gelbe* Seiten) and e-mail addresses is at: www.t-info.de

Der Spiegel The site for the major German weekly magazine Der Spiegel is at: www.spiegel.de

Current Events by City To find out what's going on in major cities, including the weather, fairs, theater, concerts, what's in the local newspapers, airline and train schedules, and any other event, go to: www.msn.de/meinestadt

For business information about Germany in both languages look in the list of Chambers of Commerce. They often have their own Web sites with links to other related sites.

DRIVING AND AUTOMOBILES

ADAC (Allgemeiner Deutscher Automobilclub)
Am Westpark 8
81360 München
Tel: (089) 76760
Web site: www.adac.de

American Automobile Association (AAA)
Heathrow, FL
Tel: (407) 444–7000
Web site: www.aaa.com
For information on driving while abroad and International Driving Permits.

Auto Exchange
Web site: www.mcs-autoexchange.com
European distributor of U.S.–specification automobiles; new cars only.

Automobile Association (AA), UK
Tel: (0) 1256–20123
Web site: www.theaa.co.uk
For information on driving while abroad and
International Driving Permits.

AvD (Automobilclub von Deutschland)
Lyonerstr. 16
60528 Frankfurt
Tel: (069) 6606–0

Canadian Automobile Association (CAA)
1145 Hunt Club Road / 1145, ch. Hunt Club
Suite / Bureau 200
Ottawa, Ontario K1V 0Y3
Canada
Tel: (613) 247–0117
Fax: (613) 247–0118
Web site: www.caa.ca
For information on driving while abroad and
International Driving Permits.

Military Sales Center
Web site: www.military-car-sales.com
Used cars, English-speaking service; 6 locations
throughout Germany.

Volvo Tourist and Diplomat Sales
Web site: www.volvo.com
New cars built to meet the specifications of your
destination country.

SCHOOLS

Bavarian International School
Tel: 08133–9170
Fax: 08133–917135
Web site: www.bis-school.com

Berlin/Brandenburg International School GmbH
Tel: (033) 208676–0
Fax: (033) 208676–12
Web site: www.bbis.de

Bonn International School
Tel: 0 2 28 30 85 40
Fax: 0 2 28 3 08 54 20
Web site: www.bis.bonn.org

European Council of International Schools (ECIS)
Web site: www.ecis.org
*General information on international schools
in Germany.*

Frankfurt International School
Tel: 0 61 71–2 02–0
Fax: 0 61 71–20 23 84
Web site: www.fis.edu

International School of Dresden
Tel: 0351–340–0428
Fax: 0351–340–0430

International School of Düsseldorf
Tel: 02 11–940 66
Fax: 02 11–408 07 74
Web site: www.isdedu.de

International School of Hamburg
Tel: 0 40–88 30 01–0
Fax: 0 40–8 81 14 05
Web site: www.international-school-hamburg.de

International School Hannover Region
Tel: 0511–537077
Fax: 0511–557934
Web site: www.is-hr.de

International School of Stuttgart
Tel: 07 11–76 96 00–0
Fax: 07 11–76 96 00 10
Web site: www.ecis.org/iss

ISF Internationale Schule Frankfurt-Rhein-Main
Tel: 069–2197–1315
Fax: 069–2197–1441

Leipzig International School e.V.
Tel: 0341 421 0574
Fax: 0341 421 2154
Web site: www.intschool-leipzig.com

Munich International School
Tel: 0 81 51–36 61 20
Fax: 0 81 51–36 61 19

TRAVEL IN GERMANY

Deutsche Bundesbahn
Web site: www.bahn.de/
Information and reservations in German and English.

CROSS-CULTURAL RESOURCES

Terra Cognita
Web site: www.terracognita.com
Videos, books, audio and Internet training and resources for living and working in Germany and around the world.

METRIC
CONVERSIONS

Although a sizing conversion chart can be a step in the right direction, an accurate fit is found only by trying the item on, just as you would at home.

WOMEN'S DRESSES AND SKIRTS

U.S.	3	5	7	9	11	12	13	14	15	16	18
Continental	36	38	38	40	40	42	42	44	44	46	46
British	8	10	11	12	13	14	15	16	17	18	20

WOMEN'S BLOUSES AND SWEATERS

U.S.	4	6	8	10	12	14	16	18	20	22	24
Continental	32	34	36	38	40	42	44	46	48	50	52
British	26	28	30	32	34	36	38	40	42	44	46

WOMEN'S SHOES

U.S.	5	6	7	8	9	10
Continental	36	37	38	39	40	41
British	$3\frac{1}{2}$	$4\frac{1}{2}$	$5\frac{1}{2}$	$6\frac{1}{2}$	$7\frac{1}{2}$	$8\frac{1}{2}$

MEN'S SUITS

U.S.	34	36	38	40	42	44	46	48
Continental	44	46	48	50	52	54	56	58
British	34	36	38	40	42	44	46	48

MEN'S SHIRTS

U.S.	14½	15	15½	16	16½	17	17½	18
Continental	37	38	39	41	42	43	44	45
British	14½	15	15½	16	16½	17	17½	18

MEN'S SHOES

U.S.	7	8	9	10	11	12	13
Continental	39½	41	42	43	44½	46	47
British	6	7	8	9	10	11	12

CHILDREN'S CLOTHING

U.S.	3	4	5	6	6x
Continental	98	104	110	116	122
British	18	20	22	24	26

CHILDREN'S SHOES

U.S.	8	9	10	11	12	13	1	2	3
Continental	24	25	27	28	29	30	32	33	34
British	7	8	9	10	11	12	13	1	2

DISTANCE

1 yard	0.914 meters
1 foot	0.305 meters
1 inch	2.54 centimeters
1 mile	1.609 kilometers

1 meter (m)	1.094 yards
1 meter (m)	3.279 feet
1 centimeter (cm)	0.394 inches
1 kilometer (km)	0.622 miles

SPEED

1 mph	1.609 km/h
30 mph	48 km/h
55 mph	88 km/h
65 mph	105 km/h
80 mph	128 km/h
100 mph	160 km/h
1 km/h	0.622 mph
55 km/h	34 mph
65 km/h	40 mph
80 km/h	50 mph
100 km/h	62 mph
150 km/h	93 mph

DRY MEASURES

1 pint	.551 liter
1 quart	1.101 liters
1 liter	0.908 dry quarts

LIQUID MEASURES

1 fluid ounce	29.57 milliliters
1 pint	0.47 liters
1 quart	0.946 liters
1 gallon	3.785 liters
1 liter	1.057 liquid quarts

WEIGHT

1 ounce	28.35 grams
1 pound	0.45 kilograms
1 gram	0.035 ounce
1 kilogram	2.20 pounds

TEMPERATURE

To convert Fahrenheit into Celsius, subtract 32, multiply by 5, and divide by 9.

To convert Celsius into Fahrenheit, multiply by 9, divide by 5, and add 32.

FAHRENHEIT → CELSIUS		CELSIUS → FAHRENHEIT	
-20	-28	-50	-58
-15	-26	-45	-49
-10	-23	-40	-40
-5	-20	-35	-31
0	-17	-30	-22
5	-15	-25	-13
10	-12	-20	-4
15	-9	-15	5
20	-6	-10	14
25	-3	-5	23
30	-1	0	32
35	1	5	41
40	4	10	50
45	7	15	59
50	10	20	68
55	12	25	77
60	15	30	86
65	18	35	95
70	21	40	104

FAHRENHEIT → CELSIUS		CELSIUS → FAHRENHEIT	
75	23	45	113
80	26	50	122
85	29	55	131
90	32	60	140
95	35	65	149
100	37	70	158
105	40	75	167
110	43	80	176
115	46	85	185
120	48	90	194
125	51	95	203
150	65	100	212
175	79	105	221
200	93	110	230
225	107	115	239
250	121	120	248
275	135	125	257
300	148	150	302
325	162	175	347
350	176	200	392
375	190	225	437
400	204	250	482
425	218	275	527
450	232	300	572

APPENDIX C